What's the single most important
I have graduated?

Shay: The most important thing to do financially is to start building up your credit and your savings. Both of these things will give you the financial foundation you want as you build your future. Chapter 2 is all about savings, and Chapter 3 gets you started on good credit habits!

Do I need to have a credit card to establish good credit?

Hallie: Having a credit card account that you manage well is a great way to establish credit. Be careful: charge only what you can afford and pay it off every month. Do this and you will start establishing great credit. Like Shay says, hit Chapter 3!

What should I do first: invest, save, or pay off my loans?

Shay: Why choose? You can pay down your debt and save for both the long and short term all at once. We'll show you how to separate your money into "buckets" and create a goal and a monthly contribution amount for each bucket.

I have my first job. How much of each paycheck should I put away?

Shay: Twenty percent of your paycheck should go to savings, and this should be split between short- and long-term savings. This is a great time of life to build up a cash reserve while you have fewer obligations and expenses than you may in the future. The habits you create now will be with you forever!

I'm thinking of buying a house. How will I know it's the right time in my financial life?

Hallie: Buying a house is about more than just the house; it's about making a good decision about a financial commitment you will have for years to come. Think about how long you plan to be in the area, how much you can afford to put down on a house, and the stability of your income. Chapter 5 will help you make the right decision.

What should I think about financially if I want to go back to school?

Hallie: the first thing to think about is *why* you are going back to school. What will the next round of schooling allow you to do that your current education will not? Does it make sense, both personally and financially, to go back to school?

I plan to get married within the next couple of years. What financial considerations come with marriage?

Shay: The first thing to do is start a conversation about money with your future spouse. Start talking about the little things, like how you choose to spend your money and why. Discuss what you're doing, and what you want to do to have a bright financial future. Then create a plan *together*.

Money FAQs

If I have the cash, is it better to pay off a student loan all at once, or over time?
Hallie: As with all financial decisions, this one is about balance. If paying off your loans all at once leaves you with no emergency savings, you may want to consider paying them over time. Commit to payments that you know you can make, then make additional payments as often as you can while still keeping your savings goals intact, too.

What's more valuable in a job offer: a high salary or good health insurance?
Shay: Both are important; look at the numbers. A company can tell you what it costs them to insure you and any dependents you may have. As with all things, know what you need and how much you are willing to pay for it. If you're in good health, a basic plan accompanied by a job with a high salary may be right for you. If you have health issues, great health insurance may offset a slightly lower salary.

What can I do now to pay less in taxes next year?
Shay and Hallie: To make sure you're handling your taxes well, look at both your tax deductions and your paycheck withholding. Are you contributing as much as you can to your retirement plan? Are you recording every charitable contribution you make? Are you withholding enough from your paycheck? Read more in Chapter 2.

When should I start saving for retirement?
Shay: NOW! Do not pass GO; start saving for retirement. Even if you only put away a small amount each month because of debt and short-term saving needs, put away *something*. In this case, a little can eventually go a very long way.

Why do I need financial power of attorney? My parents have always been able to do all these things for me.
Hallie: If you're over the age of 18, your parents cannot legally do these things for you anymore—without a financial Power of Attorney. If you want their help and want them to be able to speak to your financial institutions, get one in place *now*. There's a lot to learn here, so be sure to check out Chapter 7.

I want to buy a car. What should I know?
Shay: Before you set foot on a car lot, know exactly how much you're willing and able to pay for a car. Know how much you have for a down payment, and how much you can pay monthly. I recommend that your car loan be no more than 48 months. There are many online calculators that will help you, put in the amount you want to pay each month, the amount of time you will pay, and the interest rate and it will tell you how much the total car cost can be. Read more in Chapter 5.

Get It Together
The real-world money guide for graduates

Shannon Prosser

Hallie Hawkins

LOG CABIN BOOKS

LOG CABIN BOOKS
6607 CRAINE LAKE ROAD
HAMILTON, NY 13346
WWW.LOGCABINBOOKS.COM

COPYRIGHT © 2011 BY SHAY PROSSER AND HALLIE HAWKINS

All rights reserved. No part of this book may be reproduced, distributed,
or transmitted in any form or by any means, or stored
in a database of retrieval system without the
prior written permission of the publisher.

First Paperback Edition: May 2011
10 9 8 7 6 5 4 3 2 1

Library of Congress Control Number: 2011928741

ISBN 978-0-9755548-9-0

Cover Art by Tripp Griffin
Book Design by Eva Williams
Index by Megan McDowell

For the strong women in my life:
my grandmothers, Anna Gabor and Rose Grover;
my mother, Dot Bolton;
and my daughters, Annie and Emily Hawkins.
- *Hallie*

For the family that has supported and
encouraged me on this journey:
Johnny, Taylor, Mom, Dad, and Stacy.
- *Shay*

Contents

Chapter 1 - Your Vision, Your Life 3
- It's your life; Now, live it well! 4
- What's important to me 8
- Priorities in action 8
- Choices in life 12
- The Time-vs.-Things Challenge 13
- Choices and feelings 15
- What I've learned—and where I learned it 18

Chapter 2 - Cash, cash, and more cash 21
- Cash flow basics 22
- What comes in: the inflow 23
- Deciphering your paycheck 24
- Get more return for your return every month:
  - The 1% Rule 25
- What goes out and where it goes: the outflow 25
- Cold, hard cash flow 27
- Stop charging and take charge of your credit 32

Chapter 3 - Debt: Something Owed 41
- Debt terminology 44
- Debt - The good, the bad, and the ugly 44
- How credit works for you and against you 45
- Interest can be interesting 46
- Credit scores and you 48
- Debt management 56
- Add it up 58
- Schooling in school loans 59

Chapter 4 - The Benefits of Benefits 63
- Staying healthy 64
- Retire what? 68
- Insuring your income 71
- All about spending accounts 72

Chapter 5 - Where to live, what to drive...................................... 73
    Buying a car 74
    Insure what? 78
    Living at Home — Whose home? 81
    Renting a home 82
    The process of buying a home 84
    Key things to know about your mortgage 87

Chapter 6 - Keeping your money and investing in your future 91
    All about basic accounts 94
    Know where to hold it 98
    Five steps to investing 102
    In control, or over-controlling? 107
    Staying on track 112
    Your tolerance for risk 113

Chapter 7 - Legal Lessons for Life 119
    You're over 18. Did you know 120
    Deciding who has the power 120
    Where there's a will, there's a way 131

Epilogue 137

Index 138

Acknowledgments 140

About the Authors 141

INTRODUCTION

Get It Together was founded by two entrepreneur moms—a 30-something financial advisor and a 40-something lawyer—who joined forces during an economic crisis. As we watched so many middle-aged and elderly people struggle, we wondered how on earth today's young people would ever learn to manage their personal finances better.

An idea was born.

Our vision is to equip people of all ages with the tools to manage their money responsibly so they can be financially confident in both good times and bad.

This book combines the knowledge of these entrepreneurial moms and a very wise 20-something who, at the time this book was written, was just moving from college to the real world. We have vastly different experiences that are all wrapped up in one guide that can lead you to the life you want to live. The information you read here will help you make wise and informed decisions along the way.

The foundation of the *Get It Together* philosophy is that the choices you make today will influence the opportunities you'll have available today and tomorrow. Good choices are educated choices; educated choices lead to far-reaching opportunities. So now, get educated and *get it together*!

This book can be used a few different ways. You can read it straight through or use it section by section. Read the content and do the exercises when you are ready to focus, learn, and apply the principles. As with the rest of your life, you can do it your way.

But *do* it.

1

Your Vision, Your Life

*Your life is yours to live.
We'll walk you through exercises to figure out
where you're going—today and tomorrow.*

It's your life; Now, live it well!

What's important to me

Priorities in action

Choices in life

The Time-vs.-Things Challenge

Choices and Feelings

What I've learned—and where I learned it

It's your life; Now, live it well!

Think about it: What does the idea of 'living your life well' look like to you? In order to know what to do to live your life well, you have to know the answer to that question. You have to know what is important to you and how you want to incorporate those values into your life.

This may seem simple, but it's not. Creating a mental picture of 'a life well-lived' will help you to identify some important things about yourself that you hadn't thought of before.

Where do you see yourself in the next 1 to 2 years?
Here are some areas to think about:

Your mind — what do you want to be doing intellectually?

_____

_____

_____

Your body — how do you want to feel?

_____

_____

_____

Your spirit — how do you hope to feel about where you are and what you are doing?

_____

_____

_____

YOUR MONEY — WHERE DO YOU WANT TO BE FINANCIALLY?

___

YOUR CONNECTIONS — WHAT PERSONAL RELATIONSHIPS DO YOU WANT TO HAVE?

___

IN 5 YEARS?

___

IN 10 YEARS?

___

WHOM DO YOU SEE INVOLVED IN YOUR LIFE IN 1 TO 2 YEARS? THINK ABOUT THESE CONNECTIONS: FRIENDS, FAMILY, A SPOUSE OR PARTNER, KIDS, PETS....

___

IN 5 YEARS?

___

IN 10 YEARS?

___

It's okay if you're not the type of person who normally plans things, or if you don't have a specific vision right now; you can make spontaneous decisions and let life take you where it leads. But even if that's what you choose, you should still have the information and education to make good decisions.

These exercises will lead you to a greater understanding of what an educated decision is and how to make one—even if it's a decision you make at the spur of the moment.

WHAT DO YOU WANT TO EXPERIENCE OVER THE NEXT 10 YEARS? COLLEGE? GRAD SCHOOL? MARRIAGE? CHILDREN? TRAVEL? HOME OWNERSHIP? A NEW JOB?
LIST THE TOP THINGS YOU WANT AS THEY COME TO MIND.

_____
_____
_____
_____
_____

WHERE DO YOU WANT TO BE IN YOUR LIFE TOMORROW? DO YOU WANT TO RENT OR BUY A HOUSE OR A CAR? SAVE UP FOR A RAINY DAY? GET OUT OF DEBT?

_____
_____
_____
_____

WHAT EXPERIENCES DO YOU WANT TO HAVE RIGHT NOW? THE ABILITY TO SPEND TIME WITH FRIENDS AND FAMILY? THE ABILITY TO CONCENTRATE ON YOUR CAREER?

_____

_____

_____

_____

WHO DO YOU WANT TO KEEP OR HAVE IN YOUR LIFE RIGHT NOW? FRIENDS, FAMILY, PETS?

_____

_____

_____

_____

WHAT ORGANIZATIONS DO YOU WANT TO BE INVOLVED WITH? COMMUNITY, CAREER, RELIGIOUS?

_____

_____

_____

_____

What's Important to Me

Now you're going to pull from the information you listed on the last few pages. We'll help you put it in one place so you can see what you have listed. We'll also make sure that list is complete for your life today—and for the life you envision.

Look at your answers to the questions on the previous pages and place everything you listed in one of the categories listed.

Priorities in Action

Priorities are great. But how do they fit into your life and into your plan for the future? Knowing your priorities will allow you to make good plans and achieve your vision. Putting these priorities into action will help you fit them into your life and plan.

Now, let's take *action*. With each of these priorities, associate actions to help you achieve your goals. What are you going to do, either now or in the future, to create the life you envision?

For example, for your family, are you going to work to provide for them? Spend time with them? Send your children to school? For your charitable organization, are you going to give them your money, your time, or both? You may want to spend time with your mom now and take care of her in her old age.

Place an action you plan to do by each priority. There can be more than one thing you are going to do for, with, or because of each listing. For each priority, list at least one action.

What it is...	My priorities are...	I am going to....
The people I have or want to have around me		
The types of organizations I want to join		
The material things I have or want to have in my life — big, small, or in-between		
The experiences: what I want to do regularly, or individual adventures or experiences I want to have		
The Ideals I want to live up to in my life: what impact do I want to have in my life, for personal reward or for the good of someone else?		
Other – anything that is of utmost importance to me that is not listed anywhere else		

Creating your Vision

You are the architect of your life. Build upon what you love and believe. Now that you have considered your priorities and values, it's time to let your imagination loose!

Using words, pictures, images from the web, cut-outs from magazines, etc., you will create your personal vision board. On this page and the next, create a visual collage of the people, organizations, things, experiences and ideals that are important to *you*!

Choices in Life

The choices you make in life either get you closer to the life you want to lead—or take you further from it. With each choice, you are making a decision about the opportunities you want today AND tomorrow. A very wise person once said, "Luck is where preparation meets opportunity." Let yourself be lucky by being prepared! The reality is, many options in your life will be defined by the financial world you create. Your financial world must be aligned with your priorities to give yourself the best chance of living the life you want to lead.

CH**OPPORTUNITIES**OICES

THE TIME-VS.-THINGS CHALLENGE

Describing life as "a balancing act" is a misnomer. In order for balance to exist, the things on both sides of the scale must be in perfect alignment—for a moment, at least. Yet real life is a constant state of change. Sometimes the changes are minor; other times they're major.

There's a push and pull in life between time for living and time for work. If you are independently wealthy, you may not be subject to this particular challenge. But if you're like most of us, you either need to work or your spouse or partner needs to work just to be able to afford to live your life.

Fitting your living and work worlds together is something we call the *Time-vs.-Things Challenge*.

The more things you want or need, the less time you have to do as you please. This is a concept many people have difficulty grasping.

DETERMINING WHERE YOU LIE ON THE CONTINUUM DEPENDS ON WHERE YOU ARE IN LIFE, WHAT YOU WANT, AND WHO YOU ARE AS A PERSON.

Try to think of things in terms of how much time you want and need. Then think about how much time you need, or are willing to devote, to financing that life. In addition, understand that, as the circumstances of your life change, the Time-vs.-Things decisions you make will change. This is not a one-time decision; it's a decision you'll need to be aware of at every step, to keep your life going where you want it to go.

THE CHOICE YOU MAKE AT EVERY TURN IN THE TIME-VS.-THINGS CHALLENGE WILL HAVE A DIRECT IMPACT ON THE OPPORTUNITIES THAT ARE AVAILABLE TO YOU. IT IS PART OF MAKING CONSCIOUS CHOICES.

Today I spend my time....

Today I spend my money....

Tomorrow I would like to spend my time....

Tomorrow I would like to spend my money....

CHOICES AND FEELINGS

In life, we have a million and one choices, and nearly every one we make is accompanied by an emotional reaction. Good, bad, wonderful or awful, the feelings that go with choices cannot be ignored. We sometimes do smart things for silly reasons—or silly things for smart reasons. Whatever the case, we have to be aware of how emotions play into the decisions we make.

IT'S TIME TO DETERMINE HOW YOU FEEL ABOUT THE OPPORTUNITIES IN YOUR FUTURE. COMPLETE EACH OF THESE THOUGHTS:

I HAVE $10 IN THE BANK RIGHT NOW. I FEEL...

I HAVE $10 IN THE BANK AND BILLS DUE AND NO INCOME. I FEEL...

I HAVE A MONTH'S WORTH OF EXPENSES IN THE BANK. I FEEL...

I HAVE TO ASK MY PARENTS (SIBLING, FRIEND) FOR MONEY. I FEEL...

I'M 35 WITH 2 YEARS' SALARY SAVED UP AND NO CREDIT CARD DEBT. I FEEL...

I AM 35 AND HAVE 2 KIDS AND $100 IN THE BANK AND NO SAVINGS. I FEEL...

I WANT TO TAKE A NEW JOB THAT PAYS LESS. I HAVE SAVED FOR 15 YEARS. I FEEL...

I'M 25, WAS JUST LAID OFF, AND CAN'T PAY RENT. I FEEL...

I CAN'T BUY A HOUSE BECAUSE MY CREDIT IS BAD. I FEEL...

I JUST GOT A GREAT INTEREST RATE ON THE LOAN I NEEDED FOR MY NEW HOUSE. I FEEL...

WHEN I LOOK AT MY FINANCIAL SITUATION TODAY, I FEEL...

HABITUAL HABITS

We all have habits, and knowing your own can bring you closer to understanding what you're doing—and why. Some habits are great, some are not so great. *Beside each of the habits circle one of the numbers: 0 for never, 1 for occasionally, 2 for regularly, and 3 for always.*

1 – I buy things without looking at the price   0   1   2   3

2 – I contribute regularly to my savings   0   1   2   3

3 – I treat my friends when we are out without thinking twice about it   0   1   2   3

4 – I pay for things with the money in my regular account, or a credit card that I pay off every month   0   1   2   3

5 – I have at least one bill each month that I am late paying   0   1   2   3

6 – I think about any major purchase for a while and do research to make sure I get the best price   0   1   2   3

7 – I have services or things that I pay for that I do not use   0   1   2   3

8 – I choose entertainment that is affordable and that I can pay for with extra money   0   1   2   3

9 – I pay for things on a credit card and do not pay it off every month   0   1   2   3

10 – I pay my bills or schedule them to be paid as they come in   0   1   2   3

Look at the odd-numbered questions and add up your points.

0-5 points: Good job; you are staying away from destructive habits

6-10 points: You're doing okay, but should take a look at each of the habits that you scored 2 or 3 on and think of a way to make that habit better

11-15 points: Your habits are getting in your way. List each of the habits, and next to it, write down a new habit to replace the old one. For the next 5 days, implement one of the new habits each day until you have incorporated each of the habits into your life. Over the next month, concentrate on these new habits until they become second nature to you.

Now add up the even-numbered questions and add up your points.

0-5 points: Look at each of the habits listed and over the next 5 days implement at least one of the habits into your life. If you scored low on the even questions, you probably scored high on the odd questions. You may have a lot of habits to change, but once they become second nature, you'll be well on your way to financial fitness.

6-10 points: You have some good habits, so keep making them better! For each of the habits that you scored less than a 3, think of a way that you can get to that 3

11-15: Congratulations! You have some very good habits and are on your way!

What Matters Most

When you're in the middle of a decision, it can be difficult to weigh the options and determine what is most important. Measuring the impact of a decision is rough—so we have some tools for you.

It's easy to give yourself the go-ahead to do things you want and ignore things you don't if you are focused on today. But how do you factor in the short-, mid-, and long-term impact of your actions or non-actions?

We're going to give you a few examples, and you'll have space to write down things in your own life that are weighing on your mind.

If I choose to save the 20% of my salary that this book tells me to:
  Today, I'll have less money to spend on wants
  In a month, I'll have started learning to live on less and will have some savings
  In a year, I'll be used to living on this amount and will have a substantial savings
  In 5 years, I'll have a large amount in savings and will have opportunities I may not
      have had if I hadn't saved

If I choose to spend part of my savings on a once-in-a-lifetime experience that I really want and have thought hard about:
  Today, I'll have a great time participating in that experience
  In a month, I'll tell all of my friends and family about it and relive the experience
  In a year, I'll be glad I did it, even though I'll be rebuilding my savings
  In 5 years, I'll be thankful that I did it when I could, and I'll still have the memories

If I _____
  Today, I will
  In a month, I will
  In one year, I will
  In 5 years, I will

If I _____
  Today, I will
  In a month, I will
  In one year, I will
  In 5 years, I will

If I _____
  Today, I will
  In a month, I will
  In one year, I will
  In 5 years, I will

What I've Learned—and Where I Learned It

Feelings about money range from the slightest joy to euphoria on one side, and from a bit of shame to deep regret and depression on the other side. You can feel shame from buying even the smallest thing if you know you can't afford it. You can feel extremely proud of saving even a small amount if you know it's the right thing for you.

Understanding where you learned your ideas about money and how they make you feel can help you make better decisions. Let's look at where you came from and what you learned about money.

Who taught you about money?

- _____
- _____
- _____

What did they teach you?

- _____
- _____
- _____

What did each of them do well?

- _____
- _____
- _____

What did they do poorly?

- _____
- _____
- _____

Be honest with yourself about what each of these people did—and what you have learned from them. Think about the patterns you see in yourself that are good or bad—and *own* them. This is not about berating anyone for what they have done in the past; it's about recognizing the past for the good and bad things you learned. Most of all, it's about keeping the *good* habits in the future and getting rid of the *bad* ones.

Your money legacy is in your hands now. Make it a great legacy for yourself and the people you care about. Families have habits. Make sure you create a family with good habits.

WHAT DO YOU WANT TO KEEP DOING THAT THESE PEOPLE DID, OR THAT YOU ARE ALREADY DOING?

_____

_____

_____

_____

WHAT DO YOU WANT TO DO DIFFERENTLY?

_____

_____

_____

_____

YOU'RE RESPONSIBLE FOR *YOURSELF* NOW.

LEARN HOW TO DO THINGS WELL

AND TAKE PRIDE IN WHAT YOU DO.

2

Cash, cash, and more cash

Now it's time to start figuring out your financial life. First, we'll help you figure out where you are right now and what you're doing. Then we can look at where you want to be. We'll explain some key concepts and help you understand where they fit into your life.

Cash flow basics

What comes in: the inflow

Deciphering your paycheck

Get more return for your return every month: The 1% Rule

What goes out and where it goes: the outflow

Cold, hard cash flow

Stop charging and take charge of your credit

Just like the cycles of the ocean, the cash flows in and the cash flows out. But unlike the tides, some days your cash is primarily coming in and some days it's primarily going out. It's not in a comfortable or predictable cycle. You can't control the tides of the ocean, but you *can* have control over the flow of your cash.

If you want to know when to turn on or turn off the cash flow, you have to understand the situation you are in and anticipate the situations you might face. Know what comes in and where it goes. Sound simple? It is–if you keep track.

The first concept to understand is that what goes out must have come in from somewhere. It may come from your job, your parents, your spouse, student loans, credit card companies, a friend, or a relative. No matter how much money you have, you should know where it's coming from.

Of course, you must also know what goes *out*--and where it goes. If this thought makes you cringe, just keep reading. And if you think you have it under control, ask yourself this question: "Exactly how much do I spend each month?"

Now read the rest of this section, and complete the exercises to see if you are on target.

CASH FLOW BASICS

You should calculate your cash flow on a monthly basis for a few reasons. First, it's a short enough time-span to understand and keep track of what is going on in your finances. Second, you will incur many bills and expenses on a monthly basis. Finally, everyone can relate to a monthly schedule and can identify things that happen in different months that cause more outflow or inflow.

WHAT GOES OUT MUST HAVE COME IN – FROM SOMEWHERE....

WHAT COMES IN: THE INFLOW

To understand what comes in, you have to start with the sources of the money you receive.

WRITE A LIST OF ALL OF THE SOURCES FROM WHICH YOU HAVE RECEIVED MONEY IN THE LAST SIX MONTHS AND THE SOURCES FROM WHICH YOU EXPECT TO RECEIVE MONEY IN THE NEXT SIX MONTHS.

How Often	IN THE PAST 6 MONTHS, I HAVE RECEIVED MONEY FROM...

How Often	IN THE NEXT 6 MONTHS, I WILL RECEIVE MONEY FROM...

To the left of each of the above statements, write *how often* you have received or expect to receive money. Use the following abbreviations:

- (**M**) - Monthly – for money that you expect to receive for an indefinite period, like a salary or wage
- (**O**) - One-time- for money you will only get once
- (**Y**) - Yearly – be sure to note how many years you expect to get this
- (**S**) - Sporadically – for money you get from bonuses, overtime or other unpredictable occasions
- (**R**) - On request – for those people or places you get money from when you ask
- (**C**) - On credit – if you have used a credit card or loan that you have not paid off in full

Now we'll go further to break down the money that you earn or receive. A dollar earned is not necessarily a dollar in your pocket; your wages go through a filter that shrinks them considerably before you ever receive your paycheck. If you're starting a new job, be sure to base the planning of your personal cash flow on what really will be coming in rather than the whole salary. There are several ways you can ensure that the amount you receive is the right amount, and that you are making the best use of tax laws.

Deciphering Your Paycheck

Your pay-stub is the best place to start to see where your money goes. The key to knowing what you bring in each month from your employer is to look closely at your pay-stub. This will also help you understand which benefits you are paying for and which ones your company is providing to you for free. Now, you are ready to determine how much income you bring in each month.

List the following items that are deducted from each paycheck you receive in a month.

	Job 1	Job 2
Gross Paycheck		
Federal Taxes		
State Taxes		
Medicare		
Social Security		
Health Insurance		
Life Insurance		
Disability Insurance		
Employee Stock Purchase Plan		
Employer Retirement Plan (401(k), 403(b))		
Other (List individually)		

GET MORE RETURN FOR YOUR RETURN EVERY MONTH: THE 1% RULE

Most people are really excited when they get a large refund from the IRS. However, if your refund is too large because of this once-a-year giveback, your cash flow cycle may have been weakened throughout the rest of the year. You may have been loaning the government your money--interest free--during that time. If you have been in your current financial situation for at least one tax year, then apply the following: Look at the amount you were refunded or the amount of tax you paid when you filed your tax return last year. Now look at your income. If the amount you paid or received is more than 1% of your income, you need to do some adjusting.

If you were pleasantly surprised by a large refund, it is possible that you could have had that money 12+ months earlier! Don't let this happen again. Check your current tax withholding status and see if it can be adjusted to more adequately reflect your situation, and get more money in your pocket monthly. Online pay-stub calculators and the IRS site can help you determine how many exemptions to take.

If you paid more than 1% of your salary in taxes last year, that hurt! Adjust your withholding and have your employer withhold more. Don't get hit with an unexpected tax bill again.

If you're self-employed, work with an accountant to make sure you are filing correctly and not incurring unnecessary penalties. An accountant can also help make sure you are taking advantage of all of the appropriate allowances and provisions in the tax code.

WHAT GOES OUT AND WHERE IT GOES: THE OUTFLOW

The key to understanding what goes out is knowing where it is going and why. There are things that you *have* to pay for and things that you *want* to pay for. Then there is everything else. By accounting for each expense and categorizing the expenses, you will know what is going out and where it is going. The goal here is twofold; understanding where your money is going, and then making sure that where it is going is either necessary or meaningful. *What you spend your money on should enhance your life.* Everything from a roof over your head and heat for your home to the money you spend on leisure should add to your life in some way.

To start, you'll answer some questions and then do some analysis of your spending. Luckily, bank and credit card records can help you easily categorize and calculate your spending. If you are moving from college to a job, or from one job to another, or going through another major change, then estimate your expenses. Once you have made it to the next step, redo this exercise and make sure you know where your money is actually going.

WHAT ACCOUNT(S) DO YOU SPEND FROM?

_____

_____

_____

_____

DO YOU PAY ALL OF YOUR EXPENSES?
IF NOT, LIST WHO PAYS THEM AND IF/WHEN YOU WILL BE EXPECTED TO TAKE OVER THOSE EXPENSES.

_____

_____

_____

_____

DO YOU SPEND ON A CREDIT CARD?

_____

_____

_____

_____

Do you pay off the balance each month?

_____

_____

_____

_____

Cold, hard cash flow

Where's it all going?

Nice Save!

List the amounts you put into your savings or retirement accounts. Only list an amount in the savings category if you truly *save* it and do not take money out of your savings for day-to-day expenses.

Type of Savings	Amount Saved per Month
Savings account	
Brokerage account	
IRA	
Roth IRA	
Employer Retirement Account	
Other Savings	

If you don't know what some of these savings vehicles mean to you, you soon will. We'll discuss these concepts later and exploring why they are important to you and how they can help you reach your goals in life.

The Big Picture

In order to know what you spend, take a look at your last 3 months of expenses and put them in one of the following categories. Add up all of the expenses in each category and divide by three. Why three months and not just one? Over three months, you will incur almost all of the types of expenses you have to pay over the course of the year. This is also to make sure that it is an accurate picture, not just a snapshot of one month when you may have spent more or less than usual. Over three months, your habits are sure to appear.

The 'Have-to-Haves'

These are the things that keep a roof over your head, food in your belly, clothes on your back, and enable you to go to work.

	Month 1	Month 2	Month 3	Average
Rent or Mortgage				
Second Mortgage/ Home Equity Line/Loan				
Electricity				
Natural Gas/Oil				
Water				
Home Phone/ Cell phone basic plan				
Childcare				
Groceries				
Out-of-pocket Healthcare Expenses				

Health Insurance				
Clothing for work				
Home maintenance				
Homeowner's or Renter's Insurance				
Medicines				
Security System				
Parking at Work				
Education expenses				
Business expenses				
Property tax				
Monthly Credit Card payments				
Car loan				
Car tax				
Car maintenance				
Car fuel				
Car Insurance				

I want it! I want it!

These are the things that are great to have. You like these things and they are things that you want to have in your life, although they are not vital to everyday living. Many of these are extra purchases or activities.

	Month 1	Month 2	Month 3	Average
Cable TV				
Cell phone (upgraded plan)				
Internet Access				
Dining out (lunch)				
Dining out (dinner/weekend)				
Gifts				
Pets				
Home Décor				
Entertainment				
Vacation				
Charity				
Newspapers, Mags, and books				
Non-work clothing				
Health club				
Personal care – hair, nails, etc				
Other				

Reflections Break

WHAT'S THE BEST DECISION YOU EVER MADE INVOLVING MONEY?

WHAT'S THE WORST?

WHY WERE THESE DECISIONS GOOD OR BAD?

WHAT WOULD HAVE MADE THE BAD DECISION BETTER?

Stop charging and take charge of your credit!

Do you think you have good credit, bad credit or no credit? How do you know?

The trick with credit is that most people think they have good credit when they actually have *no* credit. To understand your own credit rating, you must know what credit is and how it is defined by the companies that issue credit.

Your personal credit is a calculation by credit-reporting agencies that tells companies how likely you are to repay any loan they may give you.

Simply speaking, credit is a debt that you owe to a person or company. They extend you credit (the ability to spend money you do not have) or give you a loan.

To define credit, we need to define the basic terms of credit and debt. In "Debt: Something Owed," we explain in detail what debt is and how it can work for or against you. When someone extends credit to you, you are in debt. A debt is simply something owed to someone or some company.

A dollar saved makes more cents

The best way to make money by doing nothing is to have the money that you have saved work to make more money. There are entire books written about how to make money work for you. We are going to start with one of the easiest and most common ways to make this happen.

Compound interest – Compound interest happens when the money you put aside to save (the principal) earns interest, and then that interest becomes principal and also earns interest.

The concept is simple: Save money. Invest that money so that it earns money. Here are the dollars and cents, working FOR you.

If you start with $100 and it earns 5% a year, at the end of the year that account is worth $105. If that account continues to earn 5% in year 2, at the end of year 2, it has earned an additional $5.25. The money earns more in the second year because there is more principal working for you.

Year	Amount invested at beginning	Amount Earned	Amount at end of year
1	$100	$5	$105
2	$105	$5	$110
3	$110	$6	$116
4	$116	$6	$122
5	$122	$6	$128
6	$128	$6	$134
7	$134	$7	$141
8	$141	$7	$148
9	$148	$7	$155
10	$155	$8	$163

If the money is left in the account and it continues to earn more money, it grows quickly.

Let's take this example one step further. Over those same 10 years, if you continue to add $100 a year, the money grows even more quickly. In this case, the total investment over the 10 years is $1000. At the end of the 10 years, it's worth over $1300.

Year	Amount invested at beginning	Amount Earned	Amount at end of year
1	$100	$5	$105
2	$205	$10	$215
3	$315	$16	$331
4	$431	$22	$453
5	$553	$28	$580
6	$680	$34	$714
7	$814	$41	$855
8	$955	$48	$1,003
9	$1,103	$55	$1,158
10	$1,258	$63	$1,321

Live today – Prepare for tomorrow

There are a lot of philosophies on whether you should live for today or save the best for tomorrow. Well, we say that is ultimately up to you – but we suggest both. It is not an 'either/or' scenario, but rather one where you can live today AND prepare for tomorrow. The key is practicing both spontaneity and planning in a way that is true to who you are.

So how much do you plan or how spontaneous are you? Do you live for today, or do you put off all of the fun until tomorrow? Come on – live life and love it both today and tomorrow, and the next day.

To balance the spontaneity and planning, you need to see how you feel about things. Think about the following topics and write down your opinions and thoughts. There can be more than one 'something' and more than one feeling about that action.

For this exercise think of larger things in life that you would like to experience, have, or enjoy. Think about your personal goals and obligations. 'Now' means in the next days, months, or year. And 'later' means in a few years or more.

Something you want to do now:

Feeling -

Something you want to do later:

Feeling –

Something you want to have now:

Feeling –

Something you want to have later:

Feeling –

Someone that you want to take care of now: (yes, this can be yourself!)

Feeling -

Someone that you want to take care of later: (yes, this can be yourself!)

Feeling –

A DOLLAR SAVED MAKES MORE CENTS

THE 80/20 RULE OF SAVING

The question of how much to save can seem like a tricky one, but it really isn't. We would all like to think that we can save just a little and be fine, but the reality is that each of us is responsible to secure his or her own future by saving money. That is why you should live by the 80/20 rule: save 20% of your income, and you can spend the other 80% (after the tax man takes his chunk out, of course). For unusual income, gifts, bonuses, etc., use the reverse rule: save 80% and you can spend 20%.

The 80/20 rule is a way to gauge how much you are saving compared to how much you are bringing in. Since almost every person brings in a different amount of money, this is the best way to see how you are doing. Now, the 20% may seem a little high to some people; the reason for this is that less of your future is going to be covered by employer pensions and social security than ever before. But if you cannot save that 20% today, at least work toward that goal. Don't use the excuse that you can't afford to save 20%—only to save nothing at all. You are responsible for your own future.

For every dollar brought in by regular income, 20% should go to savings and 80% can go to day-to-day living expenses. For every dollar brought in by windfalls or any other unexpected occurrences (like bonuses, gifts, etc.), 80% should go to savings and 20% to spend on whatever you would like. If you are in any level of credit card debt, then 100% of all windfall money should go directly to creating a reserve of 6 to 9 months of living expenses, then to credit cards.

Calculate the Amount You're Currently Saving:

(Total Monthly Savings divided by Income x 100) = % of income you're saving)

A simple way to gauge this is to multiply your total monthly savings by 5. If this number is more than your total income... congratulations. You're saving more than 20%. If this number is less than your income, you have some work to do.

How to Save and Where to Save

There are two ways to find more money to save, bring in more money, or spend less. In other words, increase the inflow or reduce the outflow.

Increase the Inflow

Most people find it is difficult to increase the amount of money that comes into their household. Here are a few options to increase the input.
- Work overtime
- Get another job
- Sell things that you don't need

Reduce the Outflow

For most people, the best way to find money to save is to reduce the outflow. This option makes the greatest difference in both your lifestyle and your bottom line. The key to reducing the outflow is to target nonessential expenditures that will make the biggest impact on your bottom line. Do not eliminate needs. Contrary to popular belief, you can often make a big impact by eliminating a few large items, rather than making many small changes. For example, getting a less expensive car and reducing your car payment by $200 a month is more effective than trying to give up a $2 cup of coffee each day for $60 a month. Do both and you have a lot more money!

On the cash flow sheet, you calculated how much you are bringing in and how much you are spending. If you are spending more than you are bringing in, note exactly how much you're overspending. That is how much you need to cut. If you are not overspending, it's still a good idea to look at where you can save. If you are spending money on things that don't matter to you, then you may be better off saving that money.

To find areas to target, go back to your cash flow sheet. Look at where you are spending money. Are you spending more in an area than you thought? To reduce spending, start with the areas that mean the least to you. These will have the least impact on your life and are the easiest areas to adjust. Then move up in importance until you reach the amount that needs to be trimmed. Track your spending as you change the patterns.

KEY AREAS TO TARGET
- Cable TV – shop TV plans and consider eliminating extra channels
- Cell phones – shop cell phone plans, review minutes actually used, and make sure the plan you have is the right one
- Automobile payments – get a cheaper car
- Entertainment – don't cut this out completely, but reduce it
- Dining Out – eat in, eat at cheaper restaurants, take advantage of special deals or offers from favorite restaurants, eat out on 'off' nights when there are specials rather than on weekends
- Clothing – shop sales and consignment stores for the absolute necessities, trade with friends, consign old clothes to pay for new ones
- Gifts – buy on sale, buy less, buy more thoughtful but less expensive gifts, create a gift exchange with friends or family members by drawing one person rather than buying for all
- Vacations – take cheaper or fewer vacations, or both
- Anything in the 'I Want it! I Want it!' section is up for grabs

WAYS TO REDUCE CURRENT EXPENSES
- Power, Natural Gas, Water – shut off lights and appliances, use resources sparingly, reduce the temperature in your hot water heater, raise the AC temperature and lower heating temperatures for thermostat. Open the windows
- Car fuel – take the bus, carpool, do errands in groups to avoid going out more times than necessary
- Groceries – eating is a necessity, but a little planning can go a long way. Buy food on sale and freeze or store, plan meals for a week and shop once rather than daily. Use coupons, shop sale fliers from local grocery store, join a produce co-op, shop a local farmers' market
- Non-reimbursed business expenses – make sure that any business expenses are necessary and are going to drive business. Anything that does not drive business should be reconsidered

Areas not to skimp on
- Health Insurance
- Life Insurance
- Car Insurance
- Home Insurance
- Childcare

Write down 5 ways you can start saving – TODAY!

Try This!

There are many things you can do to test yourself and to make sure you're making conscious decisions. You may already do some of these things, but try them again! Put a check mark next to each idea that you have tried. Then write under it how you felt when you did it. Keep this checklist around in case you're feeling weak one day and need some help remembering those feelings.

___ **The next time you're in a store or online and see something that you really want to buy, before you make that move, walk away.** Stay away for at least 24 hours, then see how you feel about the item.

When I walked away, I felt_____

When I thought about the item 24 hours later, I felt_____

___ **Think about your health, spiritual life, or something that fulfills you.**
How much time and/or money are you devoting to it each month? _____
hours/days_____dollars
How can you devote more time and/or money to it?_____
_____

___ **Go through your room or house and find 5 things to sell.** Take them to a consignment store or list them on an online auction site.
When I put them up for sale, I felt_____

___ **Collect the money that you earned from the items that you sold.**

When I got the money, I felt_____
I felt especially _____ because I used the money for _____

___ **Go through your closet, room or house and find things to give to charity.** These should be things in good working order that someone else could use. Take a look at each item and try to remember when you purchased it or how you got it. Was it something you were dying to have? Did you pay cash or put it on credit? Think about how you feel about that item now.
When I donated the items to charity, I felt _____

Recalling what the items meant to me when I got them, I remember I felt
_____

___ The next time you think about purchasing something that you feel you "have to have," think about how long you plan to have that item, and what feelings you have about that item. <u>Each item you have should enhance your life in some way.</u> If you begin a purchase by thinking about how long you will have that item, it's easier to evaluate the cost and see if it's worth it. Will you get the amount of enjoyment you want for the price you are paying?

How will you feel when that item is in the pile to go to charity?

_____

___ For the next holiday or birthday when you plan to give someone a gift, set a limit and challenge yourself to get a thoughtful gift for under that amount. We suggest that you set the limit at $20 or below.
When I gave that gift, I felt _____

___ The next time you're considering purchasing something or an experience and don't know whether it's worth the cost, don't buy it. Instead, take that money and put it into your savings OR do something for someone else with it.

When I did this, I felt_____
and it was a _____ feeling than I think I would have had with the object or experience I was going to buy.

___ Think about the things that you like to do for entertainment that are not free. How much did it cost you? _____ How can you have as much fun for less? _____

___ What in your life do you spend your time and/or money on that does not fulfill you? _____hours/days _____dollars
How can you spend less time/money on it?

_____

3

Debt: Something Owed

Debt and credit scores may seem like something you only have to be worried about if there is a problem, but that's not so. You need to have a thorough understanding of what debt is, how it's used, and what to think about when you choose to use it. Debt can be a valuable tool or your worst enemy; luckily, you can control how it affects your life.

Debt terminology

Debt - The good, the bad, and the ugly

How credit works for you and against you

Interest can be interesting

Credit scores and you

Debt management

Add it up

Schooling in school loans

This chapter covers the things you need to know about debt. It's very important that you have some basic understanding of this part of the money issue. Work your way through it; if you don't want to read in detail, at least skim it. You can come back and review the terminology when you feel the need to do so.

Quality of Life

In order to understand who you are and how you deal with things, it's good to know how you react with regard to debt. The quality of life that you have and the quality of life that you want are driven by the decisions you make. The decisions you make ultimately help you or hinder you on your way to financial freedom. You decide.

1 - When I think about the debt that I have accumulated, I feel:
____ I am drowning and I have nowhere to go, so I don't do anything
____ I have made decisions in the past that I have to live with, but I still feel guilty about them
____ I have a solid plan to get out of that situation and understand why and how I got there
____ I either have no debt or the debt that I have is worth it because of the opportunities or things that were provide by it

2 – When I think about the way I have spent money in the past, I feel:
____ I have had good reasons to spend and have spent only as much as I could afford
____ I have spent more than I can afford to, but that I do not know what else to do
____ I have a lifestyle to keep up and that I have to spend this way to do it, even if it means that I am in debt
____ I do not know where my money goes and that I am constantly scrambling to pay bills

3 – When I think about what I have spent my money on, I feel:
____ I spend what I have to for needs and have enough to also save and that I can spend money on things I want
____ I have spent lots of money on things that I want, and then have struggled to find the money to pay for the things I need, like rent/mortgage
____ I was constantly moving money around in order to find a way to justify spending money on what I want to
____ I have no idea what I have spent my money on, I just know that I never have any

4 – When I think about the debt that I have accumulated, I would like to feel like:
___ I have a plan and will get out of the situation
___ I have debt that is reasonable and I know what decisions I made that need to be improved upon, and what decisions were good ones
___ I have a plan that is working and I know when I will be done paying off the debt
___ I would like to feel exactly as I do feel

5 – When I think about the way I spend money, I would like to feel:
____ I have had good reasons to spend and that I spend only as much as I could afford
____ I have saved 20% of my income each month and that I can spend the remaining 80% on what I want and need
____ I have a lifestyle that is reasonable to keep up with the income that I have
____ I am able to pay all of my bills on time and in full, and am able to save

6 – When I think about what I spend my money on, I would like to feel:
____ I spend what I have to for needs and have enough to also save and that I can spend money on things I want
____ I spend money on things that I need and that I am also able to save
____ I have a predictable cash flow that allows me to pay things on time
____ I have a good idea where my money comes from and where it goes, and I am comfortable with my cash flow

Look at questions 1-3 and review what you have marked for these. How do you feel about those answers? Now look at 4-6 and review your answers. How do you feel about those answers?

Do you want to feel more like you did in your answers to 1-3, or your answers to 4-6? You decide.

Now let's look at debt and take action!

DEBT TERMINOLOGY

Borrower – A person or entity that is required to pay back the loan.

Lender – A bank, institution, or individual that loans money or extends credit to the borrower to purchase items.

Secured Debt – A debt that requires something of value be offered as collateral to secure the loan. Mortgages, home equity lines and loans, and car loans are examples of secured debt. If payments are not made to the lender, the lender can take possession of the collateral item. Title loans are also secured debt. In this case, the borrower offers the ownership of the car in exchange for a loan.

Unsecured Debt – A debt that does not have any item of value offered as collateral. Credit cards are the most common example of unsecured debt. The lender must sue to recover the loan if the borrower does not pay back the loan.

Revolving Debt – Credit that is extended to the borrower from the lender up to a certain limit. The amount owed varies with charges and payments made to the lender. Credit cards are revolving debt.

Installment Debt – Debt that is paid back to the lender through a series of planned payments. Mortgage and car loans are generally examples of installment debt.

Asset – Anything of value, either tangible or intangible, that has value and can be sold for cash or used to produce cash.

DEBT — THE GOOD, THE BAD AND THE UGLY

Good Debt – Debt is generally considered to be good if it meets most or all of the following conditions:
- The asset purchased has a reasonable potential to increase in value (i.e. mortgage)
- The experience purchased will justify the cost by providing opportunity (i.e. student loans)

Good Debt can easily turn into bad if any of the following are true:
- The payments are too high in relation to the income of the borrower
- The cost of the debt (usually interest payments) is too high to justify the potential increase in value of the asset or opportunity

Bad Debt – Bad debt is the kind that may be useful for cash flow purposes. The borrower should watch this type of debt carefully to make sure it does not become a burden. It is most commonly accumulated on credit cards. It can also include home equity lines of credit. This debt meets the following conditions:
- The asset purchased is expected to decrease in value
- The experience purchased is not for a greater good, such as higher education
- The item purchased is a consumable

Ugly Debt – this type of debt should be avoided because it can cause serious damage. It is important to note that we typically refrain from telling you not to do something. We believe that you should decide for yourself what is right for you. However, we are deviating from that in this instance. Do not use the ugly debt listed below!
- Title loans
- Payday advance

How Credit Works For You and Against You

Credit allows you to spend money you do not have at the time of the purchase. It also allows you to borrow against future earnings, which is basically what student loans do. The issuers of student loans know that you, as a student, have no way of repaying these loans while you are in school. They are banking on the expectation that you will get a job—and a paycheck—when you get out of school that will allow you to repay these loans. We will discuss student loans in greater detail later in this section, so remember this concept when we get to that part.

Credit can work against you in many ways:

- You can get yourself in too deep by overestimating what the object or experience you are borrowing money for is worth.

- You can get in over your head if, by borrowing against future earnings, you anticipate a higher salary than the one you actually end up receiving.

- You can use credit too easily to buy things that are not worth it. When you're not paying with cash, it is easy to overspend.

- The biggest way credit works against you is that you have to pay interest on every purchase. If you purchase a $100 item or experience at a 10% interest rate, in a year you will owe $110--and you'll have nothing more than that original item or experience purchased. So basically, you are paying a premium on every purchase rather than paying for it with cash you have. For example, you got something you really wanted and it was on sale. Such a deal! But the reality is that, over time, this item may cost you much more than the original price due to the interest you pay. Ultimately, it will not end up being such a wonderful deal.

Interest Can Be Interesting—Especially If it Works For You!

Compound interest can either be your best friend or your worst enemy. Either way you use it, it's your choice. And either way, you have to know how it works.

Compound Interest is when a dollar--either spent on credit or saved--earns or accrues interest. We are going to explain compound interest in terms of debt now, and then later in the section, we'll go into more depth about how it can work for you.

If you spend $100 on a credit card at 10% interest, at the end of the year you will owe $110—the original $100 plus $10 in interest. The next year that $100 keeps on accruing interest, but then you're also charged interest on that $10. So, by the next year you owe $100, plus the first year's $10 PLUS another $11 in interest. After two years, you owe $121 for a $100 purchase.

Now imagine your interest rate is 20% on that same $100 purchase. After one year you owe $120, and after two years you owe $144!

The interest does not usually just get piled on once a year; it accrues daily, weekly, monthly. For every day you owe the money, you owe more money.

Debt: Something Owed   47

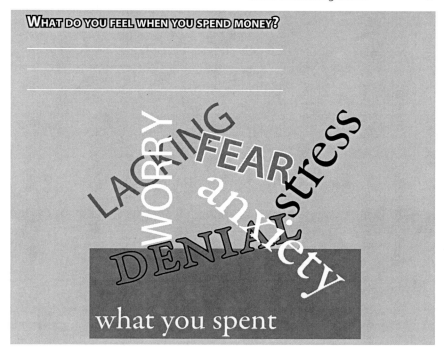

Credit Scores and You

Credit reports and credit scores used to be one of those things you didn't have to worry about. Several years ago, you might have checked your credit score when you were turned down for a credit card or loan. You may also have known you had a credit problem and wanted to begin to work at it. Money was easy to get, and the alternative was to attempt to find someone, somewhere, who would give you a line of credit. In addition, jobs were easy to find and unemployment was very low.

Credit reports are simply reports that show your potential creditors what kind of potential borrower you will be. It gives them a snapshot of your bill-paying history, how many credit accounts you have, your balances and credit limits, and when those accounts were opened. They'll check your job history, salary history, collection accounts, and more. The snapshot of your finances changes from day to day; but in general, it will stay within a certain range--unless your financial behavior changes radically.

Credit scores are regularly used for the following areas, but may be used in other areas as well. Companies are finding new, interesting ways to use your credit report as an indicator of who you are and how you handle responsibility.

Interest rates

Need a car loan or a mortgage? It might be more difficult to get those loans when you need them. Since the recession and the financial crisis, it is harder to borrow money from banks. There is a credit crunch for businesses and individuals, and for every job, there might be thousands of applicants. The ironic thing is that it is very important to have good credit during a credit crunch, but with high unemployment and underemployment, it can be difficult to maintain good credit. And you need good credit now more than ever.

Most people are aware that the credit score affects the interest rate they are offered on money they owe. There's a one word reason for this: RISK. A credit score measures risk of default based on a person's past handling of money and personal history.

A credit report does contain financial information--like whether or not you pay your bills on time, if you are late in making payments, and how often your payments are late. If you are late on making payments, are you 30 days late? 60 days late? Did you default on the loan altogether and force it into collections? Have you declared bankruptcy in the past?

It can also contain information about our lifestyle. Where have you lived? What employers have you worked for? Have you ever had a judgment against you?

> THE CREDIT REPORT ITSELF GIVES INFORMATION ONLY.
> IT'S YOUR JOB AS A CONSUMER TO MAKE SURE
> THAT THE INFORMATION IS CORRECT.

The creditors who use the credit report to pull information about you will interpret and set their own policies regarding how the credit report will be used to affect their decisions.

Employment

Besides looking at your financial world to decide what the risk is in loaning you money, companies have been pulling credit scores when looking at candidates for jobs. More and more, companies take a look at your credit score to decide if you will even be considered for employment. The laws will vary from state to state. Your resumé may be perfect, but your credit score might be a disaster. You might not be called in for the final interview. The logic is that the poor decisions you make with your money and other life choices may affect your job performance. The logic may be flawed: It may be that you have a poor credit score because you have no job or have had to take a large cut in income. Or the logic may be correct: It may be that your poor credit score reflects lack of money management skills and knowledge. Whichever is correct, be aware that your credit score might affect your employment opportunities.

Insurance Rates

Some states allow the use of credit scores to set premiums on life insurance, auto insurance and property insurance. The insurance industry can cite studies that show the credit history is directly related to claims. The lower the credit score, the higher chance that a claim will be filed with the insurance company. A lower credit score may mean higher insurance premiums. This is called a credit-based insurance score.

You need to check your credit report regularly. Again, be aware that it's critical for many more reasons than just applying for loans on a home or car.

Establishing Good Credit

You establish credit the first time your social security number 'officially' shows up in the credit world. If you have a student loan, you have established credit. If you have taken out a credit card or a small loan from a credit union, you have established credit. If you co-signed on another person's behalf, you have a credit file. It is critically important to check your report on a regular basis.

Establishing credit is a good thing--if it is done correctly. We will discuss the items that are reported by credit reporting agencies in detail. One of the items reported is the length of time you have had credit. By establishing good credit through a credit card or small loan before needing to borrow money, you may find it easier to borrow money when you need it. Of course, this account needs to be handled well, with on-time payments and without maxing out the credit limit.

Credit—when used wisely–is an effective tool to help you manage your financial life. It's important to establish credit so that it is available to you should you choose to use it.

- Open a bank account-Anyone loaning money to you will want to have a bank reference and a bank account number. It's good to have an open bank account--and it might even encourage you to save!

- Apply for a Charge Card – If you have credit available but do not feel that you will be able to resist the temptation, consider a gas card or store credit card. These cards will help you establish credit, but will alleviate the temptation of a major credit card, which can be used to buy things you can't afford.
    -If you can't get a credit card, look into a secured card. A secured card is attached to an account--usually a savings account–and credit limits are based on the amount required to be deposited into that account.
    -Make sure you use the credit card. Don't just put it away. To establish credit, you must use the credit line and pay it back on time and in full.
    -Make sure the secured credit card you choose reports to all three credit reporting agencies.
    -If you have bad credit, make sure the credit card company does not check credit to issue the card.

- Get a major credit card in your name. Before you do this, check the rates and terms of repayment. The credit line offers you get in the mail may be easily attainable, but the rates will likely be higher than the ones you can get by doing your own research.

- Stick within your budget. Do not consider credit as a raise in your income. Pay this borrowed money back right away and on time.

How to choose a credit card

We should repeat that to establish credit, you shouldn't just apply for those credit card offers that pop up online or the pre-approved credit applications that come in the mail. The interest rates can be higher. (In fact, you should opt out of receiving those offers TODAY so you won't be tempted!)

The Federal Reserve Bank is a great resource for choosing the best credit card for you. It provides definitions to critical financial terms that you need to know and understand. Some key concepts are highlighted below.

Each credit card has certain features and benefits that may make it more appealing to you as a consumer. Be aware that the same credit card that appeals to you may have different features that might make it less appealing. Do your homework and educate yourself on the features of the credit cards you are looking at. Create a list of each of the critical features of every credit card so you can compare the different options.

First, look at how you will use a credit card. Whether you will carry a balance or you will pay off your bill monthly, always look at the Annual Percentage Rate (APR). An annual percentage rate is the interest you will pay on a balance on your credit card, balance transfer, or cash advance.

If you sometimes carry a balance from month to month, you may be more interested in a card that carries a lower interest rate (or APR). If you tend to operate with cash advances, keep in mind that those interest rates are different—and usually higher--than the rates charged when you purchase something with the card.

All about the APR

What is the APR? The annual percentage rate-—APR—is the interest rate you will pay if you carry over a balance, take out a cash advance, or transfer a balance from another card.

The APR states the interest rate as a yearly rate. APRs can be confusing. Look for these possible fine points with regard to the APR:

- **Fixed or Variable APR** - In general, the fixed APR rate does not change unless the credit card company gives notice of the change. A variable APR rate can be adjusted, and is issued with the anticipation that it will be adjusted. Read the fine print.

- **Tiered APRs** - Different rates apply to different levels of the outstanding balances.
- **Penalty APR** - The APR may increase if you are late in making payments.
- **Introductory APR** - A different rate will apply after the introductory rate expires.

Other items to know and understand before signing the credit card contract include the following:

- How long is the grace period?
    - The grace period is the time before the credit card starts charging interest on a purchase.
- Always read the section of the offer with the information on methods of computing the balance. It is usually found in the section, "How is the finance charge calculated?"
- Does the card carry a minimum finance charge?
- What are the fees? Fees can include, but are not limited to:
    - annual fee
    - cash advance fee
    - balance transfer fee (there may be more than one tier of fee applied to the balance cash advance)
    - late payment fee
    - over-the-credit-limit fee
    - setup fee
    - return check fee

- What benefits does the card offer? Does the card offer airline miles, rebates, or additional warranties? These should be looked at, but are secondary to the other items listed above.

Under federal law, all solicitations and applications for credit cards must include certain key information in a disclosure box similar to the one shown. Numbers and terms are shown as examples only.

ANNUAL PERCENTAGE RATE (APR) FOR PURCHASES	2.9% UNTIL 11/1/11 AFTER THAT, **14.9%**
OTHER APRs	CASH-ADVANCE APR: 14.9% BALANCE-TRANSFER APR: 14.9% PENALTY RATE: 20.9% SEE EXPLANATION BELOW.*
VARIABLE-RATE INFORMATION	YOUR APR FOR PURCHASE TRANSACTIONS MAY VARY. THE RATE IS DETERMINED MONTHLY BY ADDING 4.9% TO THE PRIME RATE.**
GRACE PERIOD FOR REPAYMENT OF BALANCES FOR PURCHASE	25 DAYS ON AVERAGE
METHOD OF COMPUTING THE BALANCE FOR PURCHASES	AVERAGE DAILY BALANCE (EXCLUDING NEW PURCHASES)
ANNUAL FEES	NONE
MINIMUM FINANCE CHARGE	$.50

- TRANSACTION FEE FOR CASH ADVANCES: 3% OF THE AMOUNT ADVANCED
- BALANCE-TRANSFER FEE: 3% OF THE AMOUNT TRANSFERRED
- LATE-PAYMENT FEE: $25
- OVER-THE-CREDIT-LIMIT FEE: $25

* Explanation of penalty. If your payment arrives more than ten days late two times within a six-month period, the penalty rate will apply.
** The Prime Rate used to determine your APR is the rate published in the Wall Street Journal on the 10th day of the prior month.

RECENT CREDIT CARD RULE CHANGES

New credit card rules and regulations were implemented on February 22, 2010 by the federal government. Here are the things that credit card companies must tell the consumer.

Most of the increases in rates or fees must be disclosed 45 days before they take effect. If a credit card company is going to make changes that will greatly affect the terms and conditions of the terms of your credit, they must disclose this information to you.

YOUR CREDIT CARD COMPANY MUST SEND YOU A NOTICE 45 DAYS BEFORE THEY CAN:
- increase your interest rate
- change certain fees (such as annual fees, cash advance fees, and late fees) that apply to your account
- make other significant changes to the terms of your card

When you receive such a notice, you should carefully read the information to understand your options. While the credit card company issues the credit card and controls the terms and conditions, you do have choices to make when you receive the information.

You can cancel the card before the higher fees take effect. However, if you choose to cancel the card, the credit card company has the right to increase minimum payments. Canceling the card and being responsible for higher minimum payments may hurt your cash flow. Think about it and understand the consequences.

For example, they can require you to pay the balance off in five years, or they can double the percentage of your balance used to calculate your minimum payment. This will result in faster repayment than under the terms of your account.

THE COMPANY DOESN'T HAVE TO SEND YOU A 45-DAY NOTICE IF:
- You have a variable rate tied to an index; if the index goes up, the company does not have to provide notice before your rate goes up.
- Your introductory rate expires and reverts to the previously disclosed "go-to" rate;
- Your rate increases because you are in a workout agreement and you haven't made your payments as agreed.

Please note that you have already agreed to the terms and conditions and are aware of them. The credit card company has to disclose increases in rates that you are not aware of. So, read the mail and inserts from the credit card companies very carefully.

It can take a very long time to pay off credit card debt. Before these new laws went into effect, creditors would not make it clear how long it would take to pay off the amount owed. It was easier to take on debt without realizing the impact. Uncomfortable as it is, take a look at these figures on a regular basis. It will certainly help you understand the impact of compound interest and give you some control of your financial world.

The credit card companies must also educate users about minimum payments and what they mean. **Read this carefully;** the difference between minimum payments and higher payments could save you years—and hundreds, or even thousands, of dollars.

Late-payment warnings are disclosed as well. These late-payment fees can include both a late fee and an interest rate increase. Late payments will also affect your credit score; the increased cost and the negative information on your credit report can be a double-whammy.

If you get a new credit card with a fixed interest rate, your interest rate cannot be increased for one year. Of course, if you have agreed that the rate will increase in a shorter period of time, as, for example, with an introductory rate, then the rate can be increased. You have agreed to it.

If your payment is more than 60 days late, the interest rate can go up. So if your payment is late and you feel no pressure from the credit card company for the first 59 days of nonpayment, don't assume that the company is just being nice. They may increase your interest rate on day 60.

Please note that if a credit card company does increase the interest rate on your card, it will only be on the new charges and new balances.

Your credit card company will give you some options as to how to handle any charges over your credit limit. It used to be that the company would let the charge go through, and additional fees would be charged. Now, you can choose if you want to go over the credit limit and pay the fees, or if you would rather have the transaction tuned down. You have some choices, but you must communicate with your credit card company.

Other items covered in this new federal law include billing dates and payment-due dates, payment cut-off times, how the interest billing cycle is interpreted and imposed, and how payments are directed to your account. If you have questions, it's best to contact your credit card company and ask how all this works. Keep records of these conversations, including whom you spoke to, the date, and the information you received.

One stipulation in this new federal law states that if a person is under 21, he or she must be approved for a credit card based on income and ability to pay. If you are under 21 and have no income or ability to pay, you will need a co-signer to obtain credit. This will require both parties (the person under 21 and the co-signer) to approve any credit limits in writing. Please note that this might affect a person's ability to get credit--and the length of credit history.

This section gives the basics of the consumer credit rules that have changed. We're sure they will continue to adjust and change. Keep reading your mail —whether e-mail or US Mail—to find out what your credit card company is telling you.

Debt Management

Debt has become a growing concern to families. Understanding debt will be critical to you in reaching your goals. What you use the available credit to pay for is as important as how much debt you have. And remember, it is not just your debt that should matter to you; your spouse or partner's debt and credit situation are of vital importance to you. When you involve yourself with someone legally and financially, you take on their credit issues as well.

Debt can be thought of as dollars and cents in the budget, but think about debt with regard to these critical issues:
- Do you spend more than you earn, making it impossible to put a savings plan in place?
- Do you make the minimum payment on each credit card all the time, or have you maxed out the credit limit?
- Do you have more than 3 major credit cards?
- Does your credit card debt preclude you from purchasing health insurance, life insurance, or other critical items to protect your family?
- Do you find yourself arguing with your spouse or partner about money? Or, are you afraid to talk to your spouse about money at all? Do they even know about the debt?
- Do you think that bankruptcy may be an option?

You must manage your debt. Even for people who are in high-debt situations, taking control and looking at exactly what debt is owed and to whom it is owed is the first step to overcoming a debt problem. Ignoring the debt that has been incurred will make the problems harder to deal with in the future. It is essential that you face the tough issues and create and follow an action plan. Taking control of debt is stressful, but for most people, the plan and control ultimately relieve them of an enormous amount of day-to-day stress.

Bankrate.com compiles a weekly survey of the 50 largest credit card issuers. The average rate of credit cards was as follows in February 2011.

Balance Transfer Cards	15.96%
Cash Back Cards	16.58%
Variable Rate Cards	14.44%
Low-Interest Cards	10.87%

Given these statistics, credit card debt can in no way be considered good debt. The first step to begin to get out of credit card debt is to stop charging items. A halt on charging can help highlight how much is really being charged on a regular basis.

Take some credit for starting to *manage* debt rather than having it control your life. If you are managing your household cash flow with a partner, make sure they are on the same page and on board with the debt control process. Debt management has to be a team sport for those whose financial lives are combined. If one person is paying down while the other is charging, it is a losing battle.

A good way to take a look at your credit card debt before working it into your budget is to write down each credit card and the interest rate for each card. The cards that have the higher interest rate or are near the top of the credit limit should be paid off first. If you do have some savings over and above what you need for your financial cushion, pay off some of the debt. The return on saving money is generally very low compared to the savings you'll see from paying off credit card interest. Make sure you pay on time, because interest rates can increase substantially with late payments. These increases can sometimes double the interest rate.

AND REMEMBER: PAYING LESS THAN THE TOTAL BALANCE RESULTS IN ADDITIONAL INTEREST CHARGES, MAKING THE REAL COST OF THE ITEM HIGHER.

Besides credit card debt, auto loans are another area where the debt incurred might not be worth it. By investing in a new car with a loan, you are simply spending money on an item that inevitably will go down in value. A loan for an item that is going to decrease in value is not really wise. So if you need a new car, look at the cost and include that in your cash flow to see if it is affordable and smart. You may even decide that a used car is a better overall value than a new one. Either way, make sure that car will not make you put off important items in your action plan to achieve the life you want.

Add It Up

In this section, you're going to get a handle on exactly how much you owe--and to whom. First, you are going to take each card and write down the information. Then we are going to tally how much you owe. Then we are going to arrange the cards for payment.

You're going to figure out how much you can put towards this debt each month through your cash flow plan, and then start by paying the minimum on each card. Then the rest of the amount you can put toward debt each month is all going to go toward the card with the highest interest rate. You're going to knock off your debt from each of the cards, one at a time.

CREDIT CARD	CARD HOLDER	INT. RATE	TOTAL OWED	MIN. MONTHLY PAYMENT	CREDIT LIMIT
TOTAL OWED					

SCHOOLING IN SCHOOL LOANS

College, or some additional training over and above high school, can be critical to your professional advancement in life. College costs vary from community college, state colleges or universities, technical training, or private colleges. Each has its cost or investment. Many times, student loans can allow you to reach those goals. Whether you currently have student loans and may need more to complete your education, or you have none, look at student loans as an investment in your future. Because it is an investment, you need to look at the return--or what you get back.

Take a look at what you want to do with your life. What profession are you planning to go into? How much education will it take? What type of college can you afford, given the salary of that profession? If you are going to school to be an attorney, needing undergraduate and graduate loans, is it affordable to pay it off on an attorney's salary? State schools or private colleges? And is it your passion is to be a teacher? Given the salary, what can you afford to borrow? There are financial calculators that will allow you to figure out what each payment will be. Think about how much your life will be affected by paying $300 a month or $500 a month. How does it fit within your cash flow?

If you have already used the student loan programs, don't worry. Most students need to get student loans. But you are responsible to pay that debt back; That's the case even if you don't graduate or complete a program. Once you stop attending school on at least a half-time basis, the repayment must begin. Depending on the specific type of loan, payment can be required immediately upon leaving school or can be deferred for some months. Either way, when you prepare your cash flow analysis from the earlier chapter, you must plan on paying it back.

Student loans are currently required to be paid back and reported to credit reporting agencies. They are reported on your credit for 25 years. They are not dischargeable in bankruptcy, unless a hardship discharge applies. Such a discharge is rarely granted, so plan on paying it back. After all, you did borrow the money and attend college or other training programs. The lender really does not care whether you landed that dream job at your dream salary.

Although Federal Legislation in 2010 changed the student loan process to exclude many private lenders, we will be discussing private lenders, because they are a reality for those who have taken loans out in the past.

- **Direct Loan programs** are those programs that are made by the U.S. Department of Education. They include Direct Subsidized Loans and Direct Unsubsidized Loans. Direct PLUS loans, which your parents have signed for and are responsible for as well, are also part of the Direct Loan programs.
- **The Federal Family Education Loan Program**, or FFEL loans, include the Subsidized Stafford Loans and Unsubsidized Stafford Loans. FFEL PLUS loans are also included in this program. These were generally issued by private lenders.
- **Perkins Loans** are separate and distinct, and the loan payments will be made directly to the school that issued the Perkins Loan.

What type of student loan do you have?				
How much did you borrow?				
What is the interest rate?				
When does repayment start?				

Before you graduate or leave your school, make one more trip to the financial aid office and speak with an expert on what your responsibilities are for your loan repayment. They can help you understand the process. Your lender should contact you to decide what plan is best for you. Talk to them.

You may have many student loans for each semester you attended college or technical school. It can sometimes be difficult to keep up with many loan payments to different lenders at different times. Loan consolidation may help you lower interest rates or get a fixed interest rate. It may also be easier to make one payment instead of many. This may be a good option if it makes student loans easier to manage. Make sure you shop around for the right lender to do this. Do your homework and ask questions.

You'll have to choose a repayment plan. There are generally four options to handle how to repay your student loan:
- **A Standard Plan** sets up monthly payments to repay your loan within 10 years. You will make regular fixed monthly payments of principal and interest to repay the loan. This will have the highest monthly payment to add into your cash flow, but it will generally have the lowest amount of interest paid.
- **An Extended Plan** sets up monthly payments to repay your loan within a period of 10 to 30 years. You will be making regular fixed monthly payments of principal and interest over a longer period of time. This will have a lower monthly payment, but will have a larger amount of interest to be paid over time.
- **A Graduated Plan** sets up a payment plan that starts off smaller and gradually increases up to a set amount over time. The time period to pay this off is usually 10 to 30 years. This plan allows for the initial shock of getting out of school and paying your bills allowing for a lower monthly principal and interest rate to start. It is anticipated that your income will increase over time along with your payments increasing along the way.
- **An Income-Contingent Plan** sets up a payment plan based on your adjusted gross income reported to the IRS along with other circumstances. Payments can be very low, but the interest can add up over time, bringing the total balance owed to more than the original loans. Remember compound interest. Under this type of loan, if your loan is not paid off in 25 years, the loan is forgiven.

Consider having your monthly payment automatically deducted from your bank account if the company reduces the interest rate. Many companies take this option into consideration with regard to interest rates. The Department of Education has calculators to help you see how each of these programs would directly affect your situation.

If you cannot pay, don't avoid the debt. This is a situation where if you take control of the problem, you will be in much better shape. It is critical that you understand the consequences of avoiding debt payments. For instance, your late payments are reported to the credit agencies. You may even be sued by your lender for failure to pay back your debt. In some cases, professional licenses can be denied due to your lack of payment. We're not telling you this to scare you, but to help you understand that repayment of your student loans and communication with your lender is vital to your credit and career.

OPTIONS FOR WHEN YOU CANNOT PAY BACK THE DEBT INCLUDE:

Deferment (delaying) suspends your payments for up to 3 years. Depending on the loan, interest may or may not be incurred. Before you make a decision to defer, make sure you understand how it works for your loan, and whether interest is incurred during that period of time. Deferring payments may substantially increase the amount you owe. Speak to your lender about what makes you eligible for the program. Normally, factors that make you eligible for deferral include unemployment, disability, military service or economic hardship. You'll have to apply for deferment, and your deferment must be approved by your lender.

Forbearance also either postpones or reduces your payments for up to 3 years. Interest is usually incurred during that time, and your balance will subsequently increase. Your lender will generally consider this if you are in a medical or dental residency, or if you are in poor health or have some other personal circumstance that make repayment impossible. Some loans consider whether the payments are more than 20% of your income. You will still be responsible for repaying the loan.

SO YOU'RE ALREADY IN DEFAULT BECAUSE YOU DIDN'T KNOW THE CONSEQUENCES? THERE'S A PROGRAM FOR YOU, TOO!

Rehabilitation can take off all the negative information from your credit history. Speak to your lender and agree to begin making payments. Make those payments for 12 months *on time*, and you will be rehabilitated; thus, the name.

Having your student loan cancelled is possible, but not probable. Talk to your lender about what criteria need to be met for full or partial loan cancelation if your financial situation is impossible to escape. Chances are, the lenders have heard it all.

There are some jobs that may entitle you to some loan forgiveness or loan-paying assistance, depending on the state you live in. Nursing, teaching, practicing medicine, working in a non-profit agency or public service, or serving in the military are common in these programs.

Like other financial matters, student loan rules and regulations are changing. The new rules with regard to student loans were signed in 2010 and will be implemented gradually. The U.S. Department of Education is a great site to be aware of to find your answers regarding what is new with student loan laws and programs. Also, the Federal Student Loan Ombudsman is a good resource. If your lender is a private lender, you should be able to find information with regard to their policies and programs online at their Web site. *Don't be afraid to ask questions.*

4

THE BENEFITS OF BENEFITS

Knowing what an employer offers and how to use it can be
invaluable in evaluating a company before you take a job,
and appreciating a company once you're *in* a job.
Employer benefits are there for you to use, so
make sure you know what your employer offers.
We'll help you figure out
what all of these benefits mean to you.

STAYING HEALTHY

RETIRE WHAT?

INSURING YOUR INCOME

ALL ABOUT SPENDING ACCOUNTS

If the company you work for offers benefits–*any* benefits–use them! Benefits are a major factor when your employer determines your salary. Not using the benefits offered by your company is like throwing away part of your paycheck.

Benefits are offered by the company to keep you happy, healthy, and hard-working. Take the time to evaluate the benefits they offer and sign up for any and all that apply to you. If you are offered a job, be sure to ask what benefits your employer offers and how long you will need to work for the company before you are eligible for each benefit.

We'll go over typical benefits and some important questions for you to ask. Companies are always competing to offer better and more unique services, so be sure to ask your human resources department for information on all of the benefits that are available. Remember, answering your questions is part of their job.

STAYING HEALTHY

Let's talk about health insurance and why it's important—before we talk about what it is and how to choose it. Health insurance is a critical factor in your financially stability. Getting sick is expensive. Health insurance typically covers illnesses, hospitalizations, accidents, or medications. So what does this mean to you? Imagine that you break an arm while playing Frisbee. It could cost you thousands of dollars for treatment. A major medical illness could cost hundreds of thousands of dollars.

There are some new federal regulations regarding health insurance that will have a significant impact on you as a young professional. For example:
- You can now stay on your parents' health insurance plan, as a dependent on a family plan, until you turn 25. You can buy into it as a single-policy owner until you are 26.
- Beginning in 2014, everyone will be required to have some type of health insurance.

Watch for updates about new rules and regulations as this health care reform is implemented.

Now let's talk about health insurance. Health insurance is a major benefit of working for some companies. You should know how much you pay each month and what kind of coverage you're getting. If you are choosing between two or more employers, be sure to factor health insurance into your decision.

Health insurance is a basic need, and you should be covered at all times—even if you are healthy. At the same time, you should review your personal healthcare needs. Review the policies offered by an employer, including the key features of each plan. Because health insurance is so complex, this discussion will give you important concepts and questions to consider when making group insurance choices.

Many companies have group health plans that include "cafeteria" plans: just like going into a cafeteria, you can pick and choose only what you want. Your plan usually must be chosen each year during an enrollment period.

You should review your plan and your needs each year during the enrollment period.

The first consideration in reviewing a healthcare plan is looking at your medical needs—not the plan itself.

Consider the following:
- Do you regularly visit the doctor or specialist? If so, how often?
- Do you have a chronic condition?
- What are the costs of any medications you take?
- Do you anticipate getting pregnant, or is it a possibility?
- Do you prefer a specific healthcare provider?
- Do you have a spouse or dependents? Be sure to look at who is eligible for coverage under the plan.

The next consideration is the cost of health insurance. Be sure to include that cost into your monthly cash flow.

Here are some questions to ask yourself:
- What is the cost of each coverage option?
- How much can I afford to spend on health insurance?
- How much is the deductible? Do I have the funds to cover it?

The traditional view is that health insurance is there to cover all basic medical needs past a small deductible. A health insurance policy that does this can be expensive compared to a more bare-bones policy. Deductibles—the amount you are expected to pay *before* your health care plan pays—can range from very low ($50) to very high ($10,000).

Many times, a health insurance policy with a very large deductible is combined with a health savings plan. That can be a good option; it's better to have some basic health insurance for you and your family members rather than no health insurance. If you are in good health and rarely visit the doctor, you may be able to pay less in monthly premiums; but you'll have to pay more if you have a medical need.

Key considerations:
- **Deductible** - the amount that you are required to pay in medical expenses before insurance kicks in. A deductible is usually easy to understand and easy to see in the planned program. There can be an individual insured deductible and a maximum family deductible, so look for both.

- **Annual out-of-pocket maximum** - the maximum amount the insurer will require you to contribute each year toward the cost of care. You must meet the annual individual deductible and/or family deductible before the annual out-of-pocket maximum applies. Once the annual out-of-pocket maximum is reached, you should no longer be required to contribute toward the cost of care.

- **Health Savings Account (HSA)** –a special type of savings account that allows you to deposit part of your pre-tax income and use it for medical or long-term care expenses. Participants can only get an HSA if they also have qualified high-deductible health coverage.

  HSAs may be portable, meaning that you keep the accounts no matter where—or if—you work. Each plan is different, so be sure to ask if yours is portable. Some also roll over from year to year, so you can accumulate savings over time. The money in these accounts can usually cover all kinds of medical expenses, including those not covered by your high-deductible health plan—such as dental care or over-the-counter medication.

Since each state regulates health insurance, these definitions are general. Be sure to look at the details of the plan you are considering. If you're purchasing insurance on your own, we highly recommend that you use an agent to explain the differences in coverage.

Each situation is different, but listed below are several key issues to consider when choosing from the plans offered by your employer or when purchasing health insurance on your own.
- Does the health insurance cost fit into your cash flow? What is your monthly premium? How much is covered by your employer?
- Do you have a chronic medical condition or visit the doctor regularly? Make sure your conditions are covered and find out if your doctors are included in the plan.

- Review one more time what the different types of plans are. What features do they offer?
- Are there any exclusions? If you are or may become pregnant, be sure to know if pregnancy is excluded.
- Is there a difference in plan payments, and your required contributions, to in-network and out-of-network providers? Which hospitals are in your network?
- Are you required to pre-register for surgeries or hospital stays?
- Are there limitations as to coverage during travel?
- Are dental and vision plans included in your coverage?

WHAT IS COBRA?

The Consolidated Omnibus Budget Reconciliation Act ("COBRA") is a federal law that requires that if a person works for a business of 20 or more employees and leaves her job or is laid off, she can continue to get health coverage for at least 18 months. The participant is charged a higher premium than when she was working.

If you are widowed or divorced, you can get insurance under COBRA if your spouse was covered. If you were covered under a parent's group plan while you were in school, you also can continue in the plan under COBRA for a specified period of time or until you find a job that offers health insurance.

Rules on COBRA coverage can change—and have changed frequently—so refer to current information provided by COBRA. If you are leaving a job, be sure to understand what COBRA options are available to you. Before you decline COBRA, research and sign up for another healthcare plan. **You shouldn't go without health insurance coverage for even a short period of time.**

Health insurance is just one of the benefits that your company may offer. The other most common type of benefit is retirement planning. Companies are able to offer types of retirement plans that may not be available to you outside the company. Read on to find out more about how you can benefit from this benefit.

Retire What?

Retirement plans are one of the competitive benefits that companies use to differentiate themselves. Saving for the future while you are young can have a tremendous impact on the types of opportunities that are available to you later in life. Even a small amount that you set aside in your twenties for retirement can grow to be a large amount by the time you retire.

A Million-Dollar Proposition

How much do you need to save each month to reach $1 million by age 65? The answer: It depends when you start saving and how much interest you earn on that money.

With the money earning an 8% interest rate, you'll need to....
- Start saving $285 a month at age 25.
- Start saving $667 a month at age 35.
- Start saving $1686 a month at age 45.
- Start saving $5430 a month at age 55.

Employer Retirement Plans and You

There are two main types of retirement plans: defined benefit plans and defined contribution plans. Defined benefit plans are paid for by your employer and provide you with a specific benefit at retirement. You have no control over these plans and they are less commonly used now than the defined contribution plan. Some employers still offer both plans, so be sure to look at the details of all plans for which you are eligible or may become eligible. Ask if you don't understand which is being offered.

We're going to concentrate on the defined contribution plan, which you probably know better by the account name 401(k) or 403(b) plan. There are several versions of the plan, so we are going to speak in general about retirement plans and how they work. We'll include basic concepts you should know—and questions to ask about your plan.

How Defined Contribution Retirement Plans Work

There are two main types of plans: the traditional and the Roth. Since the 401(k) is the most common of these plans, we will refer to the plan throughout this section as a 401(k). If your plan is a different type, be sure to understand the details of the plan.

With a traditional 401(k), the money is taken from your paycheck by your employer and deposited in the account. The money is considered by the IRS as pre-tax money. You do not have to pay income tax on the money you put into this plan as long as you do not put in more than the limit that year. The amount you can contribute to the plan varies from year to year, so check the IRS website or ask your plan administrator what the limit is for that year.

With a Roth 401(k), the process of putting money into the account is the same, but you pay income tax on the money you put in the account that year. You can contribute to both a Roth and a traditional 401(k) in the same year, but you still must not put in more than the limit for that year.

Employers often match the money you put into your retirement account. Most matching programs are a percentage of what you put into your account. In other words, your employer will pay you money if you save for retirement. Free Money!

Example

Let's say that your employer's matching policy is that they will match half of what you put in. If you make $40,000 and you put 10% of your income into the 401(k), you will put in $4,000 and since the employer matches 50% of the money you put in, they will put in $2,000. Often that money comes with a little catch. You have to stay at the company for a certain amount of time to get all of the money. This is called 'vesting'. Basically, the company is trying to encourage you to stay with them longer.

A vesting schedule, or the time it takes for you to get all of the matching money, often looks like this.

Graduated Vesting

Years with the company	Percentage of match you get if you leave
2	20%
3	40%
4	60%
5	80%
6	100%

Cliff Vesting

Less than 3 years of service - 0% Vested
At least 3 years of service - 100% Vested

If you leave at any time, you always get 100% of the money you put into the plan. The vesting *only* applies to the money the company puts into your account.

How the Money is Invested

In most plans, you are responsible for choosing how these contributions are invested and deciding how much to contribute from your paycheck through deductions. The value of your account depends on how much you and your employer each put in, and how well the investments in your account perform. When you retire, you are in control of the money in your account, including the contributions and investment gains or losses. To learn more about investing your money wisely, read the investing section of this book.

The Good Side of Saving in a Retirement Plan

Money that you put into a retirement plan is for the long term. The money in these accounts has special privileges and is shielded from taxes while it is in this account. You can transfer and consolidate accounts, but it must remain in a retirement account to enjoy these privileges. The biggest advantage of both traditional and Roth retirement accounts is tax-deferred accumulation.

Tax-deferred accumulation is the ability of your money to grow without being taxed while it is growing. If you save in a brokerage account or in a savings account, you are charged capital gains or income tax on any money that you earn in those accounts. In a tax-deferred account, you are not charged capital gains or income tax on any gains, as long as the money stays in the account. You are charged at your current tax rate when you take money from the account.

The Downside of Saving in a Retirement Plan

As we have said, this is money put aside for the long term. As the current law defines it, the long term is when you are 59 ½ years old or older. Teachers and some other professionals may be able to begin using their retirement accounts without penalty at age 55. If you choose to take money out of your retirement account, you may have to pay a penalty in addition to income tax on that money. There are certain exceptions, but they are for specific circumstances. It is important to build up an emergency fund so that you will not be tempted to take money out of your retirement plan.

Other Investment Programs Through Your Employer

- **Employee stock ownership plans** (ESOP) allow you to buy the stock of your company, generally at a discount. Companies will often set up these plans so that you can directly invest a percentage of your income into your company's stock. They usually save this money for you each paycheck and then buy stock at a defined discount at a preset date. For example, they may save your money from January 1st to June 31st, then buy stock from that account on July 15th.

- **Profit-sharing plans** allow the employer each year to determine how much to contribute to the plan (out of profits or other sources) in cash or in the company's stock. The plan contains a formula for allocating the annual contribution among participants. As with any plan, be sure you read the information and understand what your company offers. Generally, you have no control over this account, but it can be very beneficial—especially if you work for a company that is growing or making money.

Please note that the examples listed here are general; they don't apply to every plan, and they don't cover any sort of government plan. It's up to you to make sure you understand the specifics of your plan. Each plan has an administrator who is there to answer your questions, so be sure to call and ask questions! These plans are called 'benefits' for a reason, so use them to *your* benefit. Each plan will provide specific information about the plan and your investment options. Read the materials so you'll have a basic understanding of the information.

INSURING YOUR INCOME

You hear about insuring your house, your car, your jewelry, your pets. You name it; there is insurance for it. But what about income insurance? Why don't you hear about that? Isn't your income what makes it possible for you to have a roof over your head and food to eat?

Well, income insurance doesn't go by that name. In fact, it goes by a couple of different names and serves different purposes.

DISABILITY INSURANCE

Disability insurance is essentially income insurance. Disability insurance is a way to make sure that if you are not able to work due to an illness or injury, you have an income coming in. Many companies offer a basic level of disability insurance to their employees. And most people don't look at this or appreciate it unless they are unable to work.

Look at your disability insurance plan now and decide if it will be enough to sustain you and your dependents if you aren't able to work.

LIFE INSURANCE

Life insurance is a way to insure your income as well. Life insurance is intended to be a way to continue taking care of the people who depend on you if you were to die. This sounds harsh, but death is a reality. If you aren't there to take care of the people you love, then the money will be there to help support them.

Life insurance may seem unnecessary if you are young and don't have a spouse, partner, or children. But it's worth considering *now*. In short, insurance companies like to insure young, healthy people because they are statistically less likely to die. By getting insurance through your company or on your own when you are young, you can have peace of mind knowing that you will be insured as you age and perhaps develop health problems. By starting young, you may earn lower premiums as you grow older. You may not have anyone who relies on you today, but that may change in the future.

If your company offers life and disability insurance, be sure to sign up. They are generally inexpensive through group plans, and they're extremely valuable if you need them.

All About Spending Accounts

Spending accounts are a great resource that companies offer to employees. They are a way to save for and sometimes reduce taxes on the money you spend on responsibilities. Some types of spending accounts are healthcare savings accounts, dependent care savings accounts, and transportation savings accounts.

These accounts allow you to save pre-tax money and then use that money for specified expenses. For example, if you have a healthcare savings account, you can save money in that account out of your paycheck. Then, when you go to the doctor and have to pay a co-pay for the visit, you can take money out of that account to repay yourself. How each account works and what it covers is specific to your plan, so be sure to understand how it works before saving or spending from the account. It can save you a significant amount of money.

If you think your co-pays, medications, and out-of-pocket healthcare are going to amount to $500 in a year, you can have that amount taken out of your paychecks—a little at a time—and put into the account. Generally, you will not be taxed on that $500. Then when you use the $500, it pays for those expenses. If you chose not to use the account and still had $500 in expenses and you were in a 25% tax bracket, you would have to make $600 to receive the $450 you need in your paycheck to cover those expenses. In other words, you would have to make $150 more dollars to cover the same bills. That's the benefit of a pre-tax plan.

Vacation is a Benefit!

Vacation is the most underrated and often overlooked benefit of a job. Take a look at your employer's vacation policy. Make sure you know how vacation is accumulated—and when it has to be used.

5

WHERE TO LIVE, WHAT TO DRIVE

When you graduate from school and enter
the working world, or in some other way become
an independent adult, the world can seem very complicated.

BUYING A CAR

INSURE WHAT?

LIVING AT HOME — *WHOSE* HOME?

RENTING A HOME

THE PROCESS OF BUYING A HOME

KEY THINGS TO KNOW ABOUT YOUR MORTGAGE

Buying a Car

Car loans are similar to the mortgages described previously. There are lots of ways to get a car – just look at the TV, there is a new ad about the car you can buy for the low, low price at every commercial break. But is that low, low price really that low? And is it really that good for you?

There are multiple options on how to get a car, our favorite of which is to get the car outright—with cash. But since many people are not able to do that, we are going to go over the most common options – leasing a car and buying a car with an automobile loan.

Lease versus Buy

To be able to decide whether to lease or buy, you need to understand the difference and also know how each transaction works. Cars generally do not go up in value as they age, so for the sake of the explanations below we will assume that the value of your car goes down the longer you have it. Cars also go down in value as they have increased mileage and wear and tear. Things that go down in value are commonly called depreciating assets.

Buying outright: pay with cash that you have, receive the title (proof of ownership) to the car from the old owner. Since a car is a depreciating asset buying can be a wise choice since it is a one time cost, and you know exactly what the cost is. When you buy the car outright, you have the full authority to do whatever you would like with the car. You can drive it as many miles as you want, you can sell it, you can do whatever. It is yours.

Buying with financing: usually through a car loan from a bank or from the dealer. The title is sent to the financing company and then when the car is paid off they send you the title.

Buying a car with a car loan may be a necessity because you do not have the money to buy the car outright. We do have to note here that it is generally unwise to buy any depreciating asset with a loan. In essence, you are paying interest as the value of the car is going down. So if you are paying 10% in interest and the car value is going down at 10% a year, then on a $10,000 loan after a year, you will have paid $11,000 for something that is now worth $9,000. Doesn't seem like the best deal, does it? The only reason we do not call this a very bad idea is that for many people (you may be included in this) a car is necessary to get to work and to live life. You need to keep this in mind when deciding exactly how much you are going to spend on a car.

How car loans work

Car loans work as we described above in the amortization section. A typical car loan is 4-6 years. We recommend that you finance a car for 5 years or less. If you cannot afford the payment for a loan that is under 5 years then you should consider a less expensive car.

When you finance a car, you pay for the cost of the car plus the interest for the loan. As with the house example later in this chapter, the total cost of the car is more than just the price you pay.

For example: If you buy a car for $15,000 and get a loan for 4 years (48 months) at 9%, you will pay a total of $17,917 for that $15,000 loan.

Months of Ownership	Total Monthly Payments	Principal Paid this Month	Interest Paid this Month	Ending Principal Balance
12	$373.28	$283.12	$90.16	$11,738.27
24	$373.28	$309.68	$63.60	$8,170.58
36	$373.28	$338.73	$34.55	$4,268.20
48	$373.04	$370.26	$2.78	$0.00

Calculations provided by Dinkytown.net

Now consider *this:* You buy the same car for $15,000, but you finance it for 7 years (84 months). Your monthly payments will be $241, but you will pay $20,272 over the life of the loan. And in addition you will be paying off principal much more slowly than in the 4 year loan.

Months of Ownership	Total Monthly Payments	Principal Paid this Month	Interest Paid this Month	Ending Principal Balance
12	$241.34	$139.88	$101.46	$13,388.51
24	$241.34	$153.00	$88.34	$11,625.86
36	$241.34	$167.35	$73.99	$9,697.87
48	$241.34	$183.05	$58.29	$7,589.02
60	$241.34	$200.22	$41.12	$5,282.34
72	$241.34	$219.00	$22.34	$2,759.29
84	$240.89	$239.10	$1.79	$0.00

Calculations provided by Dinkytown.net

When you consider the fact that a car is a depreciating asset, the amount of principal you owe is a very big deal. Using the loan examples shown consider what would happen if a $15,000 car you bought is worth $8,000 after you have driven it for three years. Which loan would be better for you to have?

If you want to sell the car after three years for $8000, you will have to pay the lender the principal balance in order to sell the car. If you had the 4 year loan you would sell the car for $8000, pay the lender $4268 and pocket the $3732 difference. If you had the 7 year loan you would sell the car for $8000 and still have to pay $9697 to the lender, so you would have to PAY an additional $1697 to sell the car.

Lenders don't care if the engine does not work anymore and you need a new car. You are obligated to pay the debt even if the car stops working.

In this example, for the 7-year loan, you would be upside down in the car loan. As with home loans, being upside down means you owe more than the car is worth. Your risk of becoming upside down in a car increases when you lengthen the amount of time for the loan. In other words, a shorter loan length means that you're less likely to be upside down.

Another way to reduce your risk of becoming upside down in a loan is to put more money down on the car. This is money that you have saved and you are not paying interest on. No matter how much your car costs, we do suggest that you put some money down on the car. We suggest this both because it is wise financially and also because it is wise emotionally. When you have to put money down, you think more about it and take more time to make a decision.

How much car to buy

The best way to figure out how much you can spend on a car is to do the math. Start with your cash flow sheet and see exactly how much you can afford and want to spend each month. Do not forget to set aside some money for automobile taxes, maintenance, insurance and gas. Come up with a reasonable amount of money you can afford to spend on your monthly car payment. Then go to an online calculator and put in the amount of money you will spend monthly, the interest rate you can expect to get (you can research current interest rates online as well) and the length of the loan (which should be under 60 months). Most calculators will give you a total amount you can afford.

Determine this number BEFORE you start looking at cars. Make this number the maximum you will spend and do not let yourself be talked into a more expensive car. Remember that more expensive cars generally cost more to insure and cost you more in automobile taxes and insurance.

A car salesman will ask you how much you can afford each month on monthly payments. The real questions are: How much can you afford to spend monthly on payments after looking at your cash flow? And how long do you want to make payments?

Leasing a car

Leasing a car is another way to have a car. In a lease you do not own the car, which has both advantages and disadvantages. You are generally restricted in ways you can use or put wear and tear on a car without paying more. You are also not obligated to pay the full value of the car if you choose not to buy the car at the end of the lease.

Leases have many details, but in general, here is how they work:

A dealer leases you a car and you agree to pay them a monthly payment for a certain amount of months. Typically you pay them a down payment on the car when you begin the lease in addition to the monthly payment. You sign a contact, and at the end of that lease, you may either turn the car in or buy the car for an amount that is specified in the original lease agreement. There are specific terms in most leases, and if you violate any of the terms you may have to pay money when you turn the car in, even if you choose not to buy the car.

Terms of the lease

- Mileage: this is the amount of miles you are able to drive the car each year. If you go over the allotted mileage you have to pay for the amount of miles you go over. You do not get anything paid back to you if you drive less than the allotted miles.
- Purchase: you can purchase the car at the end of the lease for the amount specified in the contract. You will have to come up with the cash or financing to buy the car at this point.

Why people lease cars

Leases are good for people that feel that they must have a new car every couple of years. They are also a way to have a car that is more expensive than you can afford to buy. Leases are not good for people that drive more than the allotted mileage every year. They are also not good for people that are particularly hard on cars since you may be penalized if the car is not in excellent condition.

If you do choose to lease, make sure you understand why you are leasing. And understand EVERY detail of the lease. Leases can be tricky and hard to understand. It's a long commitment and a lot of money if you make a mistake.

Reread the part in buying a car about paying for a depreciating asset. You can end up paying a lot of money for something that is worth much less than it was.

INSURE WHAT?

Insurance is one of those necessities in life that most people do not like to think about. But in this area a little thought and a little legwork can go a very long way. First, you need to understand exactly what insurance is and what it does. Insurance is a way of paying a company to assume the risk of something happening. You pay them a premium (payment), and then if any of the accidents, incidents and misfortunes listed in the policy (the contract between you and the company) happen, the insurance company pays the agreed-upon amount.

Sounds simple, right? It *is*—as long as you know what you are paying for. We have mentioned insurance in other parts of this book, but here we will go over all of the major types of insurance and let you know what to consider when deciding whether to purchase. Some insurance is optional . Other insurance, like automobile insurance, is mandated by the state in which you live.

Insurance Does:
- Take the risk of a loss off of you and place it on the insurer
- Cover as much or as little of a potential loss as you and the insurer agree to
- Cover uncertain events

Insurance Does Not:
- Cover events not stated in the policy

The basics of insurance coverage

Deductible – this is the amount of the damage that you have to pay before the insurance company will start paying. For example, supposing you have a $250 deductible and get in a wreck where there is $2000 worth of damage to your car. You will have to pay $250 , and then the insurance company will pay the additional $1750.

Policy – the printed contract issued to the policy owner which sets forth and states the terms of coverage.

Premium – the amount you pay monthly or annually for the insurance.

Coverage amount – the amount the policy will pay if something happens to the insured. There can be several coverage amounts on the policy outlining what the insurance company will pay for certain events.

Policy Owner – this is the person who owns and is responsible for making sure the premium is paid on the policy.

Insured – the person or property for which an insurance policy is issued.

Insuring Your Things

You should consider insuring against events that would be devastating to your life or financial situation if they happened. You should also consider insuring those things that would be financially difficult to replace if damaged or lost.

Things to consider covering:
- Home
- Personal Property
- Automobiles
- Collections or valuables

Homeowner's Insurance

WHAT IS IT? Homeowners Insurance generally covers the house, including the garage and other structures. It will also cover personal property within the home. Make sure you consider coverage to replace the cost of replacing the structure. There are many clauses in a policy, but the Loss of Use clause is critical. This provides the policyholder with reimbursement for extra cost of living expenses while a home is being restored. The policy may also provide for protection for accidental injuries that someone may incur while on the property. There are many types of homeowners insurance available from the broadest coverage to ones that are more limited. There will also be listed exclusions in the policy that should be discussed and understood. Take time to meet with your insurance advisor so that you understand exactly what is covered.

WHY IS IT NEEDED? Your home and your property in your home may constitute much of your assets. In order to protect your financial condition, it is best that you protect the property from unforeseen events. The cost is minimal compared to the potential loss.

Renter's Insurance

WHAT IS IT? This is similar to homeowners insurance but it is for the renter only. The renter does not need to insure the property itself. The renter is concerned with protecting his or her personal property. As with homeowner's insurance, some Loss of Use coverage is offered and third party liability can be covered. The renter's property is generally not covered under the property owners homeowner's insurance policy. If someone is renting in a long-term care facility, renter's insurance should be considered. All renters should consider having renter's insurance to cover personal property.

WHY IS IT NEEDED? To protect your assets.

Flood Insurance

WHAT IS IT? Flood insurance is offered by the National Flood Insurance Program, a federal government program. Flood insurance is generally EXCLUDED under a homeowner's insurance policy. If the property owned is in a flood zone, the coverage will be offered.

WHY IS IT NEEDED? Since floods are generally not covered under most insurance policies, it is a good idea to check to see if your property is in a flood zone. It is not necessary for all homeowners to have this coverage. You can determine if you feel the need for this coverage.

Earthquake Insurance

WHAT IS IT? Earthquake damage is generally excluded under a homeowner's insurance policy. If property is near a fault line or in an earthquake-prone area, this coverage should be considered.

WHY IS IT NEEDED? To provide protection of the investment in real estate and the property in the home.

Automobile Insurance

WHAT IS IT? Auto Insurance is required by state law when one owns a car. Each state has different laws detailing required coverage. Other coverage is optional. Some examples of automobile insurance coverage include bodily injury for injuries caused to another person or Personal Injury Protection (PIP) for coverage of injuries to the driver or passenger in the automobile. Collision coverage is available for damage to the automobile from an accident. Property damage covers damage to someone else's property. Uninsured motorist coverage handles situations with an uninsured motorist or when a hit-and-run accident occurs.

WHY IS IT NEEDED? Basic automobile insurance is required by law. A more comprehensive policy should be considered, depending on the particular situation. The more assets to protect, the more complex coverage should be considered. Premiums will vary depending on coverage and deductible, age, driving record, and many other factors.

Umbrella Insurance

WHAT IS IT? This insurance coverage is an "additional" insurance, meaning that this pays after the underlying insurance has paid out. If you have anything risky that happens at your home or that you are responsible for you should consider umbrella insurance.

WHERE WILL YOU LIVE?

There are so many options to consider when deciding where to live. Should you rent an apartment? Buy a house? Live with your parents? It seems that if you make the right decisions, life will be great. The wrong choices might lead to a life you don't envision for yourself.

As you have learned throughout this book, there is no one 'right' answer. And one decision, even if it's not the best, will not destroy your life. It's all about making educated decisions that are the best ones for your personal situation.

There are a few things we all have to deal with–a roof over our heads and transportation. This is what we are going to cover now–starting with the roof over your head.

LIVING

Deciding where and how to live is a very big decision. You might decide to follow your dreams and move to the place where you have always imagined living. Or you might choose to stay in your hometown--and in your childhood home. It's a decision that may have long-term ramifications or very short-term ones. We'll cover the basic decisions you have to think about in each of these three scenarios.
- Living at 'Home'
- Renting
- Buying

LIVING AT HOME – *WHOSE* HOME?

Living at a parent's or relative's home is becoming more and more common for young adults. Financially it may seem great, but dig deeper and see if it's really right for you. Also, consider the people who own the house.

Questions to ask yourself:
- How long will I be here? Minimum, maximum amount of time
- Why am I deciding to live at someone else's home?
- What are the pros of living here?
- What are the cons?
- How is my being here affecting the others who live here?
- How will my life be different by living at home?

Questions to ask the heads of the house:
- How long are you willing, or happy, to have me here?
- What are your financial expectations of me?
- How much do you expect me to contribute to work around the house?
- How do you feel about this situation?

Have a conversation and set expectations. As difficult as that might be, it will reduce the chances of tension later. Remember to ask these questions of EACH person in charge of the house; one person may welcome you home and think it is a great idea when the other person has a different view. Whatever their views are, you need to know them and be respectful of those views. You may consider your parent's house your house, but do they consider it your house, too?

Renting a Home

Renting can be a great option, especially as you are starting out. Renting can be a relatively short-term commitment that allows you to try out a living situation. Renting may allow you to live with other people and possibly to live in an area where you may not want to, or be able to, purchase a house. Some of the same questions you asked your parents about living at home might apply to roommates. There are some key things to consider when renting a home—and by home, we mean house or apartment—whatever the style of home you want.

With whom will I live?
- Consider who—if anyone--will be living with you. Identify the issues that may come up, and set ground rules for how to handle them. For example, who is going to be responsible for paying the rent? Whose name will be on all of the utility accounts? Is everyone listed on the rental agreement and responsible for the same costs?

What is the ideal setup?
- Consider location, layout, outside features, and safety. Think about your life, what your schedule is or will be, and make sure the setup works for you.

How long am I willing to commit to this arrangement?
- A typical rental agreement will last a year or more. Make sure you are willing to live there for the whole time; otherwise, it could cost you.

How much money will I need to have before I move in?
- A typical rental agreement will require some sort of down payment along with the first month's rent. Know where this money is coming from, and have it before you sign the lease.

From whom am I renting?
- Make sure that you are renting from a reputable person or company, and that you sign a lease. It's in your best interest—and in the owner's best interest—to have everything in writing.

What's in the lease?
- READ THE CONTRACT! Know exactly what you are signing. You should know your obligations, including what notice you must give if you move out. Also know what the owner or rental agency is responsible for. It is your duty as a renter to notify them when they need to fulfill an obligation in their contract, such as a repair. If you are obligated to pay rent by contract and fail to do so, a landlord can get a judgment against you and it will show up on your credit report.

Do I have rental insurance?
- Make sure you have renter's insurance to cover your things. The landlord's homeowner's insurance policy covers the house itself, but generally, not your belongings. So protect yourself from losing everything.

What are my rights as a tenant?
- You do have rights as a tenant. Legal protections are in place to make sure you're treated fairly. People or companies that rent out property on a regular basis are covered under both federal and state statutes. You cannot be discriminated against when looking for rental property, but people who are renting out space in their homes or who rent fewer than 4 units, they are not covered by this law. Also, housing that is designated as 'senior housing' or offered by a non-profit organization generally is not covered under this law. **The federal law in this area is the Fair Housing Act of 1968 and Fair Housing Amendments Act of 1988. State laws go under different names.**

YOU HAVE RIGHTS AS A TENANT IN MANY AREAS. SOME AREAS ARE LISTED BELOW, BUT THERE ARE MORE PROTECTIONS DETAILED IN FEDERAL AND STATE LAWS.

- If you are denied the rental due to credit issues, you have a right to be told the reason you have been denied.
- You have a right to live in a "habitable" place. This means it must be a decent place to live. Think running water, heat, safe conditions, and more.
- You have a right to live in a home that is free of lead-based paint.

To buy or not to buy?
Buying a home is a big undertaking, especially your first home. Just like the first time you do anything, you really won't know what you are getting into until you do it. Although owning a home may on the surface seem like a great way to make some money, you have to consider all of the angles. You must think through the key areas of your life and see how buying a home may or may not fit.

We'll go over:
- What to consider in relation to your career
- What to know about the process
- What to think about financially
- What to think about legally

Your life and career
Is it really the right time to buy?

If you're just getting out of high school or college, buying a home might be a temptation. Rates may be low and incentives may be out there. People may say that buying your first house is a great investment. But think again: buying a house is also a big commitment.

When you sign a mortgage contract, it's an obligation to pay. The mortgage company will expect payment--whether you have a job or not. Think about how steady your employment is.

When you own a home, you're tied to a community. Moving means selling before you can take that perfect job or take that promotion across country. If you decide to pursue more education, it may end up being in another state. Owning a home might limit your choices. Buying a home at the right time is a good idea; the key is determining when that right time is.

Benefits of home ownership to YOU
· Potential tax incentives
· Potential that the home will be worth more after a few years
· Potential to develop deep roots in the community

THE PROCESS OF BUYING A HOME

The Money
The first step in figuring out whether or not to buy a house is to really understand the financial aspects of owning a home. Too often, people look at the rent they pay and think that they can have a house for the same amount--or less. What a deal! While that may be true, they may not be thinking about the other aspects of owning a home.

When you rent, you can call the landlord when something breaks. When you own, it's up to you to pay for the repair. Repairs can range from small, inexpensive fixes to large, expensive ones, like the heat or air conditioning breaking down. You need to have savings in the bank to pay for unexpected expenses when you own a home. Also, there are times in your life when owning a home can be more of a burden and ultimately limit your choices.

Saving for a Home

Use the cash flow sheets in the cash section of this book to figure out how much you can afford to spend each month on a mortgage. When you look at the cash flow, you need to consider more than just the mortgage payment. Consider the PITI (principal-interest-taxes-insurance) you'll have to pay. The amount that you determine that you can afford will need to cover the mortgage payments (principal-interest-taxes-insurance) plus homeowner's association dues, and any other expenses you are obligated to pay.

There's a good Loan Estimator calculator at http://www.ginniemae.gov that can help you estimate how much it would cost to own a home. Make sure that the number you use in your cash flow is realistic.

Once you have determined that you'd like to buy a house, you have to have a down payment and an emergency fund. Don't even start looking for houses until you have these ready to go. Sure, check out different areas that might be interesting to live in. But until you have money saved, serious house-hunting may lead to disappointment. The emergency fund should be at least 3 to 6 months of mortgage payments; it should also include 3 to 6 months of living expenses.

Getting a Mortgage

Once you have saved, start looking for a mortgage professional. A mortgage is a loan that you take out for a house. We'll review the basic types of mortgages later in this section. But first, start thinking about the money. We know what you're thinking, "Why would I look for a mortgage professional before I even have a realtor?" Well, what good is it to go shopping for houses if you're not sure you can get a loan?

The best way to know if you can get a loan is to talk to the professionals who help people get loans. You may think you can get a loan, but you'd be surprised how hard it can be. A mortgage professional can help you get prequalified for a loan. He'll run your credit and see if there are any issues that need to be addressed. And no credit is not good credit; she'll also let you know how much a lender is likely to loan you.

Please note: this is not necessarily the amount you can *afford*! YOU have to determine how much you can afford. The mortgage companies are in the business of lending money and making money off of the interest you pay. They are not in the business of telling you what you can and can't afford. The number they give you is the amount they would be willing to lend you, and it's often more than you can afford due to your lifestyle. A good mortgage professional can help you figure it all out, but you must run through the numbers they give you in your cash flow analysis. See the dollars and cents that work for you.

Finding your house!

This step can be a lot of fun; you get to see different houses and decide what you do or don't want, and what your money can buy. Find a great real estate agent who knows the market you're interested in and can assist you in understanding the home-buying process. It's a critical piece of the puzzle; it'll make your life easier. No matter how tempting it may be, do NOT look at homes that cost more than you can afford. Stay in your price range, and ignore anyone who tries to talk you into buying a more expensive home. Remember, when you get that house, you're going to want to fix things up and make it yours. You'll need money to do that. Be careful not to put yourself in a position to be 'house-poor'—when you have that dream house but can't afford to furnish it, or have friends over, or do much else because your mortgage is too high.

Closing the deal

So, you've found the house that you're ready to buy, and you're pre-qualified for a mortgage. What now?

Once you've made the offer, you need to make sure you have secured that mortgage. Go back to your mortgage professional and start working on the details. You will have to do many things after signing the contract to purchase your home. These tasks will usually include:
- waiting for your offer to be accepted
- having a home inspection
- reviewing the inspection report and deciding if new negotiations need to be made
- getting all of your documentation to your mortgage professional
- meeting deadlines
- going to closing at an escrow office or attorneys office

Shopping for a mortgage

Getting back to the details of the mortgage, we do mean *shopping* for a mortgage. This is a BIG purchase, and you should be a smart consumer and shop around to find out who is going to give you the best terms AND the best service. That said, once you have decided on a lender, stop shopping and let the lender do its work. If you do your research on loans while you're looking for houses, you'll be ready to go when you find that home and make an offer.

Types of mortgages

The mortgage industry is constantly changing and coming up with new and different kinds of loans to meet the needs of different buyers. We are going to define the basic types of mortgages, and who they are designed for. We'll also give you an overview of how loans work–and they probably don't work the way you think they do, so keep reading!

These are the basic types of mortgages offered to buyers. A great thing to remember when getting a mortgage is that if you do not understand it and ALL of its terms and conditions, you shouldn't agree to it. This is probably the largest purchase you'll ever make, so make sure you know what you're signing up for. We believe that for most people, the simpler the mortgage, the better. Let an expert help you with what each loan means and how it affects you.

BELOW ARE SOME DEFINITIONS YOU NEED TO KNOW WHEN LOOKING FOR A MORTGAGE.

Fixed-Rate Mortgages – In this type of mortgage, the interest rate and payment remain constant for the life of the loan. Most common are the 10-, 15-, or 30-year, fixed-rate conventional mortgages.

Interest-Only Loans – In the first years of these loans, only the interest is paid back to the lender through the regular payments. There is usually some stipulation as to when the borrower must begin to pay back the principal of the loan.

Adjustable-Rate Mortgages (ARM) – In these mortgages, the interest rate varies based on an underlying index. It may move up or down monthly, semi-annually or annually, or it may remain fixed for a period of time, depending on the terms of the loan.

Combination Loans – These loans are fixed for a period of time, then convert to an adjustable rate--or vice-versa.

FHA Loans - These mortgages are insured by the government. An FHA loan may require a lower down-payment than a non-FHA loan. These loans may also be subject to home price limits.

VA Loans – These loans are available to veterans of the U.S. Armed Services. The federal government guarantees the loans.

KEY THINGS TO KNOW ABOUT YOUR MORTGAGE

Interest rate – this is the amount of interest the lender charges you.

Interest rate changes – you should know if the interest rate can, or will, change at any time during the loan. For example, if you get a mortgage with an ARM, the interest rate will change at the end of the designated time.

Monthly payment – know what your monthly payment will be and if that is subject to change at any time.

Additional items in the payment – know exactly what is covered in your monthly payment. Does it include homeowner's insurance or property taxes?

Private Mortgage Insurance (PMI) – know if you are paying PMI and also know how long you will be paying the extra charge.

Length of loan – this is how many years it will take you to pay off the loan.

Any unique details or features of the loan – if there is anything additional that the lender offers, make sure you fully understand the details.

What to think about legally
Buying a home with someone else

Buying a home with someone else can seem like a great idea--at the time. Many people decide to purchase a home, then get married or make a legal commitment. Determining whether it is a good plan depends on a lot of things. Only you can decide, but here are things to think about.

- What is your relationship with the person you are buying with?
- Why are you buying a home with someone else? Is it to make the mortgage payments lower? Or is it because you plan to live together long-term?
- What would happen if owning a home together should not work out?
- What would happen if something changed in your life or the other person's life, like getting a job out of town?
- Who is going to be responsible for maintenance?
- Do you have the money for maintenance?
- How are you going to maintain and furnish the home?
- Do you have the same ideas on furnishing and keeping up the home?

I SHOULD BUY THIS HOUSE WITH _____ **BECAUSE...**

_____

I SHOULD *NOT* BUY THIS HOUSE WITH _____ **BECAUSE....**

_____

It depends on the situation, and how much you talk through things before you buy. Remember, this is a legal obligation you're entering together. If you choose to buy a home with someone, and then you break up or have a falling out, it can be very difficult to get out of the legal tie that you have to each other–and harder still to figure out who gets the house!

How Mortgages work

A mortgage is often a type of loan called an 'amortized' loan. Why should you care what kind of loan you have? You should care a lot! The type of loan you have is very important, since it is the way the lender determines how

much of your payment goes to pay interest and how much of it goes to pay off the loan principal. First, let's start with some basic loan terms:
- **Principal:** this is the amount you borrowed.
- **Interest:** this is what you owe the lender for using the money. The interest rate is given in an amount called the APR.
- **APR** (Annual Percentage Rate): this is the percentage rate the lender charges you each year to borrow money.
- **Amortization:** a process by which the loan payment is applied to the principal and to the interest payment of a loan. With each payment, a portion of the payment is applied to paying off the principal and a portion is applied to paying off the interest.
- **Amortization Table:** a chart that shows, with each payment, how much is applied to each the principal and the interest.
- **Amortization schedule:** the amount of each payment that is applied to principal and to interest for your particular loan. Each loan has a schedule that will change if principal payments are made.

The amount of money you pay in interest over the life of a loan is determined by the rate at which you pay back the principal. If you pay back the principal ahead of schedule, the overall amount of interest you will pay decreases.

example

You buy a home for $110,000 and put down $10,000 on the house. The total amount of your mortgage is $100,000. You decide to get a 30-year, fixed-rate loan, and you're given an interest rate of 5%.
- Monthly payment - $536.82
- Total amount paid over 30 years - $193,256.49
- Interest paid over 30 years: $93,256.49

	Total Yearly Payments	Principal Paid This Year	Interest Paid This Year	Ending Principal Balance This Year
Year 1	$6,441.84	$1,475.34	$4,966.50	$98,524.66
Year 5	$6,441.84	$1,801.25	$4,640.59	$91,828.81
Year 10	$6,441.84	$2,311.64	$4,130.20	$81,342.28
Year 15	$6,441.84	$2,966.67	$3,475.17	$67,884.28
Year 20	$6,441.84	$3,807.29	$2,634.55	$50,612.89
Year 25	$6,441.84	$4,886.10	$1,555.74	$28,447.50
Year 30	$6,443.13	$6,271.95	$171.18	$0.00

6

KEEPING YOUR MONEY AND INVESTING IN YOUR FUTURE

So now, you know how to save money.
But where do you put it?
That's where your saving strategy
starts to become more interesting.

ALL ABOUT BASIC ACCOUNTS

KNOW WHERE TO HOLD IT

FIVE STEPS TO INVESTING

IN CONTROL, OR OVER-CONTROLLING?

STAYING ON TRACK

YOUR TOLERANCE FOR RISK

SERENITY NOW AND LATER — A STRUCTURED APPROACH

Preparation for what you think may happen—and for the unexpected—depends on faith in your techniques. None of us know for sure what is going to happen in 5 minutes, let alone in 5 years. But that can't stop us from trying to make the best decisions we know how for ourselves. In order to make decisions for the long term, you have to be in the mindset that allows you to have some patience. This may come naturally to you, and it may not. Patience and structure will lead you to serenity and security.

How patient and deliberate are you in your approach to money?

1 - I balance my checkbook on a regular basis .   T   F

2 – I know how much money I have in savings.   T   F

3 – I knew approximately how much money was going in and out of my accounts each month before even doing the cash flow plan in this book.
    T   F

4 – I rebalance my investment portfolio on a schedule.   T   F

5 – I save for things that I know I want, and then purchase them when I have enough money.   T   F

6 – I research and find the best deal I can on the things and experiences I buy.   T   F

7 – I am not afraid to do things that I don't necessarily want to if I know it is for a good reason (like buying insurance or signing a Healthcare Power of Attorney).   T   F

8 – I rarely feel remorse about money I have spent.   T   F

9 – I look at my retirement and investment accounts at least every week.   T   F

10 – I get scared when I look at my investments or savings and they have not changed significantly or have declined in a months' time.   T   F

11 – I tend to change things in my life the minute I feel they are not going the way I planned .   T   F

12 - I SPLURGE ON THINGS AND THEN FIGURE OUT WHERE THE MONEY IS GOING TO COME FROM LATER. T F

13 – I FEEL I NEED TO LIVE THE LIFE OF MY DREAMS TODAY, NO MATTER WHAT THE CONSEQUENCES LATER. T F

14 – I AM STILL PAYING FOR THINGS ON MY CREDIT CARD THAT I HAVE ALREADY USED AND GOTTEN RID OF. T F

15 – I FEEL I SHOULD DRIVE THE CAR, BUY THE CLOTHES, TAKE THE VACATIONS, ETC. NOW AND NOT WAIT UNTIL I CAN AFFORD THEM. T F

16 – I WANT MORE THAN I CAN AFFORD AND WILL GO TO LENGTHS TO GET THOSE THINGS NOW. T F

How many TRUE statements did you have in the first 8 statements?

1-2: YOU MAY NEED A LITTLE BIT MORE DISCIPLINE IN YOUR FINANCIAL LIFE.

3-5: YOU'RE DOING OKAY, BUT LOOK AT THE STATEMENTS YOU MARKED FALSE AND MAKE A COMMITMENT TO YOURSELF TO PAY MORE ATTENTION TO THESE AREAS.

6-8: CONGRATULATIONS. YOU ARE DISCIPLINED IN YOUR FINANCIAL AND LEGAL LIFE.

How many FALSE statements did you have in statements 9-16?

1-2: YOU MAY NEED TO LEARN TO BE MORE PATIENT IN YOUR FINANCIAL LIFE.

3-5: YOU HAVE SOME PATIENCE, BUT SHOULD KEEP IN MIND THAT FINANCIAL GOALS TAKE TIME TO REACH.

6-8: CONGRATULATIONS. YOU HAVE PATIENCE WITH YOUR FINANCIAL PROGRESS AND WILL SEE THE BENEFITS IN THE LONG RUN.

The first steps to good money management involve managing your personal cash flow and accumulating an emergency fund. The more in-depth strategy is when you have more than day-to-day money: more savings and long-term savings.

This section is both a reference and a guide. Read it straight through and then go back to areas that particularly interest you. There are a lot of overlapping terms and ideas to understand. Remember, it takes some people years to understand what kinds of accounts and investments are out there. Give yourself some time to let this all sink in and make sense to you, and to determine how it fits into your life.

TO TAKE CONTROL OF YOUR FINANCIAL LIFE, YOU HAVE TO HAVE A BASIC UNDERSTANDING OF THESE CONCEPTS; SO KEEP READING IT OVER UNTIL IT ALL SINKS IN!

ALL ABOUT BASIC ACCOUNTS

CHECK OUT CHECKING ACCOUNTS

A checking account is a basic account that lets you put money in and take money out. This may sound simple, but as you will see when we explore other accounts, not all types of accounts let you do this whenever you want. Most checking accounts pay little or no interest, but offer you a good bit of freedom. They can be a good place to keep your money and manage your cash flow. When deciding where to open your account, call two or three banks and inquire about the fees, the minimum deposit amount and the minimum balance you are required to keep. Be sure to ask about any special features of each account.

It's a good idea to have an account that will let you pay bills online. This is an effective way to keep track of your bills and make sure they are paid on time. A great way to manage your bills is to schedule them to be paid on or before the due date as soon as you get them in the mail or in your online inbox. That way they are paid when due, and you only have to deal with them once.

STUDENT CHECKING ACCOUNTS are a useful type of account when you are in school. They usually offer low minimum balances and low to no fees. Make sure to ask if the bank has a student account program.

OVERDRAFT PROTECTION is another feature of many checking accounts. We highly recommend that you do not spend down to your last dollar, but we also know that this can happen. Keeping a close eye on your checking account by checking your balance regularly and keeping track of the outstanding bills and checks are the best way to know how much money you have to spend. Overdraft protection is there to help you in case you do overdraw your account.

Many banks have a program where you can draw money directly from your savings account if you overdraw your checking. This means you have to have money in your savings account. Another feature will pay the amount you charged plus an overdraft fee. These fees tend to be rather large, and can accumulate quickly. Be sure you know all of the details of your bank's overdraft policies--and do your best to avoid using them.

We recommend that you opt out of overdraft protection that will cover your purchases and then charge you a fee. The temporary embarrassment that you may feel when your card is denied may be easier to handle than the overdraft charges you would face. But as always, it is up to you.

SAVINGS ACCOUNTS

Savings accounts are literally a place to park your money. They generally pay a low interest rate and have few special features. Their benefit is that they are a safe place to keep your money, and you have access to it whenever you need it. The more you keep in savings, the more the bank is likely to pay you in interest. When researching banks, be sure to tell the representative how much you have in savings to get the account with the highest possible return.

MONEY MARKET ACCOUNTS (MMA)

A money market deposit account is a type of savings account that earns interest and usually limits the customer to a certain number of transactions within a stated time period. Money market accounts usually pay higher interest rates than the savings and checking accounts at the same bank. They can be a great way to earn more on your savings, as long as you do not need to get into your savings regularly--something you shouldn't need to do if you are managing your cash flow well.

CERTIFICATES OF DEPOSIT (CD)

A CD is a product that is basically an agreement with the bank. You agree to keep your money in the CD for a specific amount of time, from a few weeks to several years. The bank agrees to pay you a higher interest rate than you would get in their checking or savings account. If you keep the money in for at least as long as agreed, you get the interest. If you take the money out early, you sacrifice some of the interest and may have to pay a penalty. CDs are

offered with a wide range of choices, so be sure to shop around and make sure of the following:
- The bank that you are purchasing the CD from is FDIC insured
- What your interest rate is and if that rate will change
- The maturation date of the CD
- Whether there is a penalty for taking the money out early, and what that penalty is
- Will the CD automatically renew at maturity? In other words, will the money be reinvested in a new CD with a new maturity date? If so, what will the rate be at the renewal?

The Federal Deposit Insurance Corporation (FDIC)

When you're choosing where to hold your money, it's important to know who is holding that money. Savings, checking and other deposit accounts, when combined, are generally insured to $250,000 per depositor in each bank or thrift that the FDIC insures. Always be sure that any institution that you do business with is FDIC-insured; in the event that they go out of business, your money will be covered. Please note that this insurance applies to the cash you have; it does not apply to the stocks, bonds, mutual funds and other investments we cover later in this section.

INVESTING IN YOUR FUTURE

Now we'll move on to investment accounts and strategies. Investing is something that can be a lot of fun–when you're making money. And it can be very boring when you need to just hold on and wait and let the market do its work. In the commercials on TV and in the get-rich-quick books, there is always a way to do things faster, easier and with better results—or so it seems. In reality, you need to understand what you are investing in and have a realistic idea of how long it may take for those investments to pay off.

IN THIS SECTION, WE'RE GOING TO TALK ABOUT INVESTING IN THE STOCK AND BOND MARKETS AS WELL AS IN CASH. THERE ARE MANY MORE AREAS THAT YOU COULD CHOOSE TO INVEST IN, SUCH AS REAL ESTATE, BUSINESSES, AND COMMODITIES LIKE GOLD AND SILVER. FOR ANY INVESTMENT YOU CHOOSE TO MAKE, YOU SHOULD CONSIDER THE BASIC PRINCIPLES WE GO THROUGH.

Think, for a moment, about the word 'invest'. According to Merriam-Webster's Dictionary, to invest is "to commit [money] in order to earn a financial return or to make use of for future benefits or advantages." If you think of this definition, you have to remember that the word "future" is used for a reason. When talking about investing, the future does not mean tomorrow or later this week. It means years down the road.

To make sure your investments have a good chance of doing what you want them to do, you need to know the rules of investing.

WE'LL COVER THE FOLLOWING CONCEPTS:

- Know where to hold it - Where to put your investments

- The Five Steps to Investing
    - Know where you are going – have a goal
    - Risk and Reward
    - How they work: stocks, bonds, mutual funds, ETFs and Annuities
    - Have a strategy for investing your money
    - Patience pays off

- Investing News – what is in the media

- Know about the tax man

Know Where to Hold It

The account in which you hold your money is as important as the type of investments you choose to buy and sell. There are very specific benefits and drawbacks to the way certain accounts and investments are taxed, and what you are able to hold in each kind of account.

Investment Tax basics

Taxes are a very important part of investing. To make educated choices about where and when to put your money into an investment, you must explore the possible tax consequences. We will explain taxes more in detail later in this section, but here are a few things to know now in order to understand the accounts.

First, you must know when you can make or lose money on an investment. You can make money by selling the investment for more than you paid, or by earning a dividend, or by earning interest. You can lose money by selling an investment for less than you paid, or by the investment becoming worthless.

- **Capital Gain** – when you sell an investment for more than you paid for it
- **Capital Loss** – when you sell an investment for less than you paid for it
- **Dividend** – when an investment pays you cash from the earnings of the company
- **Interest** – the money you are paid for holding an investment or holding your money in a certain account

The types of accounts in which you will want to hold your money are also dependent on tax decisions. There are two basic types of taxation when it comes to the accounts themselves:

- **Fully taxable** – in this kind of an account, every time you make money through capital gains, dividends, interest, or other income, that income is subject to a tax

- **Tax-deferred** – in this kind of account, when you make money on your money, it is not subject to a tax

Tax-deferred investing can be very helpful to you when you are trying to make money with your money. We will explain more about how tax-deferred investing can help you later in this section. First, you must understand the kinds of accounts available and the investments themselves.

FIVE MAIN ACCOUNT TYPES

- **Checking**– this is your primary account that you use to manage your cash flow. We suggest that you use this account to deposit your income and to pay bills.

- **Savings or money market**– these are short-term savings accounts. We suggest that you hold your emergency fund in this type of an account, preferably one that will give you a competitive interest rate.

- **Investment account** – also called a brokerage account, this is for longer-term savings. We suggest that you use this account for savings that you will not need for a year or more. This kind of account offers you investment options that are not available in a savings or checking account. You can put in money and take it out at any time. You can hold stocks, bonds, cash, CDs, ETFs, and alternative investments within it. However, be aware that any gains that made on investments within this account may be subject to income and/or capital-gains tax.

- **Pay-tax-later retirement accounts** – the retirement accounts where you put in money that has not yet been taxed. You will pay taxes on the money when you take it out of the account.
  These accounts include the following:
  - 401k (or a 403b for non-profits and teachers) that are available through many employers.
  - IRA or Traditional – Most people think IRA stands for Individual Retirement Account, but it actually stands for Individual Retirement *Arrangement*. We like to think of it as an arrangement between you and the IRS that says that if you follow certain guidelines as outlined in the tax code, you will receive special tax benefits.
  - There are other retirement accounts such as a SEP, Simple, and Keogh

  There are some key benefits and limitations of these types of accounts:
  - Your money grows tax-deferred.
  - People under 70 ½ can contribute pre-tax money up to a limit in these accounts each year that they are eligible. You must have earned income equal to or greater than the contribution amount that year to be eligible. A spousal IRA is also available for a spouse who does not work.
  - You can contribute to both a 401K and an IRA in the same year as long as you meet the income requirements for the IRS.
  - Contributions are tax-deductible for 401Ks for all tax brackets and for IRAs under current tax limits. Check with the IRS or a CPA to determine if your contributions are tax-deductible.

- When you reach a certain age, you can take the money out and be taxed at your current income tax rate at the distribution. Currently, money can be taken out at 59 ½.
- If you take money out before you are 59 ½, it may be subject to taxes plus a penalty, usually 10%.
- You may be able to take money out without a penalty if you experience extreme financial hardship, are making a down payment for a home, or are putting the money toward educational expenses. Before you take any money out, talk to an accountant to ensure your eligibility.
- You must start taking money out at 70 ½ and must take the required minimum distribution (RMD). The RMD is a calculation made by the IRS that tells you how much you must take out of your account each year.

- **Pay-tax-now retirement accounts** – the retirement accounts where you invest previously taxed money. You may not have to pay taxes when you take the money out of the account.

  These accounts include the following:
  - Roth IRA
  - Roth 401k or Roth 403b

There are some key benefits and limitations of these types of accounts:
- Your money grows tax-deferred
- You must have earned income equal to or greater than the contribution amount that year to be eligible. A spousal IRA is also available for a spouse that does not work.
- You can contribute to both a Roth and Traditional IRA in the same year, but you cannot exceed the contribution limit for the combined amount. The same holds true for contributions to a Roth 401K and a Traditional 401k. You can contribute to both types of accounts in the same year as long as the combined contributions do not exceed the contribution limit for that year.
- Eligibility for a Roth IRA is subject to income limits.
- Earnings are tax-free if withdrawn after age 59 ½ and if the account has been open for 5 years or more.
- Contributions can be withdrawn tax-free and penalty-free at any time, but you may have to pay taxes and penalty on any earnings you withdraw.
- You may be able to withdraw money without a penalty if you use the money to purchase your first home or to pay for educational expenses, or if you have a hardship.
- Before you take money out, make sure you're eligible. Talk to an accountant.
- There is no required minimum distribution (RMD) at any age for a Roth IRA.

WHAT TO KNOW ABOUT YOUR ACCOUNTS

	CHECKING AND SAVINGS	INVESTMENT ACCOUNT	PAY-TAX-LATER RETIREMENT ACCOUNTS	PAY-TAX-NOW RETIREMENT ACCOUNTS
WHAT IS IT CALLED?	SAVINGS, CHECKING	BROKERAGE ACCOUNT	IRA, 401(K), 403 (B), KEOGH, SEP, SIMPLE	ROTH IRA, ROTH 401 (K)
HOW DOES MONEY GET INTO IT?	WHEN YOU PUT MONEY IN IT	WHEN YOU PUT MONEY IN IT	WHEN YOU OR YOUR EMPLOYER PUT MONEY INTO THE ACCOUNT, UP TO THE LIMIT FOR THAT YEAR AND YOUR AGE	WHEN YOU OR YOUR EMPLOYER PUT MONEY INTO THE ACCOUNT, UP TO THE LIMIT FOR THAT YEAR AND YOUR AGE
WHEN CAN I GET TO IT?	ANYTIME	ANYTIME	WHEN YOU TURN 59 1/2 OR ARE ELIGIBLE FOR A UNIQUE CIRCUMSTANCE	WHEN YOU TURN 59 1/2 FOR ANY GAINS, CONTRIBUTIONS CAN BE TAKEN OUT ANY TIME
WHAT CAN IT HOLD?	CASH	CASH, STOCKS, BONDS, CDS—ANY INVESTMENT YOU CAN BUY	STOCKS, BONDS, MUTUAL FUNDS, ETFS, ANNUITIES AND A SMALL VARIETY OF OTHER INVESTMENTS DEEMED SUITABLE FOR RETIREMENT ACCOUNTS	STOCKS, BONDS, MUTUAL FUNDS, ETFS, ANNUITIES AND A SMALL VARIETY OF OTHER INVESTMENTS DEEMED SUITABLE FOR RETIREMENT ACCOUNTS
WHEN IS IT TAXED?	WHEN YOU EARN INTEREST, THAT INTEREST CAN BE TAXED	WHEN YOU EARN INTEREST, RECEIVE A DIVIDEND, OR SELL AN INVESTMENT FOR A GAIN	WHEN YOU TAKE MONEY OUT	THE GAINS ARE NOT TAXED; THE MONEY YOU PUT IN WAS ALREADY TAXED
WHAT MAKES IT GREAT?	MONEY IS SAFE AND AVAILABLE	YOU CAN ACCESS YOUR MONEY ANY TIME	YOUR MONEY GROWS TAX-DEFERRED	YOUR MONEY GROWS TAX-DEFERRED
WHAT MAKES IT NOT-SO-GREAT?	THE MONEY GROWS AT A SLOW PACE	THERE ARE NO TAX ADVANTAGES	BEING TAXED WHEN YOU TAKE MONEY OUT; 10% PENALTY FOR EARLY WITHDRAWAL	10% PENALTY FOR EARLY WITHDRAWAL

FIVE STEPS TO INVESTING
- Know where you are going – have a goal
- Risk and Reward
- How they work – stocks, bonds, mutual funds, ETFs and annuities
- Have a strategy for investing your money
- Patience pays off

STEP 1 - KNOW WHERE YOU ARE GOING
Set clear and achievable goals. In order to achieve your goals, you must include a timeline so you know how long you have to achieve them. Make sure that your goals are clear to you and that they are meaningful. The more they mean to you, the harder you will work to achieve them.

STEP 2 – RISK AND REWARD
One of the most important financial decisions you will make is deciding how much risk to take with the money you devote to each investment goal.

Defining Risk
Risk is the potential that you will lose some or all of the investment. Risk and reward are generally tightly connected or correlated. In other words, the more risk you take, the more potential reward there should be.

ALL INVESTMENTS ARE SUBJECT TO RISK. EVEN CASH HAS ITS OWN SET OF RISKS.
The main risks investors incur:
- **Investment Risk or Market Risk**– the risk that the investment loses some or all of the money you originally invested or that it does not grow at the expected rate for the amount of risk taken.
- **Inflation Risk** – the risk that the money does not grow at a rate that keeps up with the rate of inflation. Basically, this is the risk that the money cannot buy the same amount as it could when originally invested.

'Risk' should really be called the potential for loss – and the potential for very *rapid* loss. And 'Return' should be called the potential for gain, and the potential for *more rapid* gain.

STEP 3- HOW THEY WORK
We'll describe what investments are typically available, how they work, and how to use them. The main investment options include the following:
Stocks
Bonds
Cash Instruments
Mutual Funds
Exchange-Traded Funds (ETFs)
Annuities

- STOCK

    What is it?

    Stock is an ownership interest in a specific company. This is also referred to as equity. Stock is sold in shares. A company is divided up into a specific number of shares, and those shares are sold to the public on a stock exchange.

    How do they make money?

    Investors purchase stock to become a part owner of a company that they think is going to grow and/or is going to have a steady income that will give them a return on investment. To make money on a stock, the value of the company has to increase. Stocks increase in value when there are people willing to buy the shares at a higher price. Conversely, stock prices decrease when people are willing to pay less for the shares. In reality, there are only two times when an investor makes money owning a stock: when the stock pays a dividend and when the investor sells the stock. Dividends are a payment of the company's earnings to shareholders.

    What are the potential risks?

    Owning stock in a company is risky because the investor participates in the increases and decreases in the value of that stock. News about the company—whether accurate or rumor—can affect the price of the stock. When an investor purchases a stock, there are no guarantees that the price will go either way. If the stock pays a dividend, there is also no guarantee that it will continue to pay that dividend. Shares of stock can fluctuate for all sorts of reasons. There are no guarantees in stocks; the value of a stock can go to zero. We have all seen this happen with some high-profile companies in the past.

    What are the potential rewards?

    Of all the investments we are going to talk about, the stock market as a whole has the highest documented returns. So if you are interested in investing for a long time and can deal with volatility, owning stock in the right companies or funds can be a good long-term investment.

    Types of Stock

    Stocks exist in many different categories that we will discuss further in our diversification section.

- BONDS

    What are they?

    A bond is a loan to a government entity, organization, or company. Bonds are issued or sold by the US government, foreign governments, cities, states, and companies. Bonds are IOUs; the issuer promises to pay back the face amount on the maturity date, and often guarantees a fixed interest rate while the investor holds the bond.

How do they make money?

Bonds pay the investor by way of periodic interest payments. Then, following a specific period of time (maturity), the investor receives the initial investment back.

What are the potential risks?

Bonds are subject to three main types of risk:

- **Default risk**-the risk that the issuer does not pay the loan back. In the case of the federal government, this risk is considered low because they control the money market. In the case of cities and states, the risk is higher because the bonds are backed by the full faith and credit and the ability to collect taxes of the city or state. They can still default. For companies, the risk is higher because the company has the risk of going out of business. Related to default risk is credit risk—that the corporation or government entity the investor loaned the money to becomes a worse risk while the investor owns the bond than it was when the investor initially purchased it. Usually, this risk results in the issuer being downgraded by a rating agency.
- **Market risk**-the risk that the bond will not be worth as much as the investor paid for it if the investor needs to sell it in the bond market before maturity. Bonds cannot always be sold when the investor needs money for a price that is near what the investor paid for them. The bond market is ruled by interest rates and by the credit market.
- **Inflation risk**- the interest payment on the bond is lower than inflation, so the investor is losing purchasing power by having the initial investment tied up in the bond. $100 today does not buy nearly as much as it did in 1990.

What are the potential rewards?

Bonds can offer a relatively safe place to invest money for long-term income and the return of principal.

- **CASH INSTRUMENT**

What is it?

A cash instrument is an investment that keeps money safe and available, but produces little or no income or growth. Cash instruments are generally money market funds, CDs (certificates of deposit), and very short-term Treasury bills.

How do they make money?

Cash Instruments make money by the interest they pay. They generally pay income consistent with current interest rates.

What are the potential risks?

- **Liquidity risk** - the risk is that money is committed in a CD for a period of time and the investor needs to take that money out and cannot do so
- **Inflation risk** – the risk that money loses purchasing power
- **Opportunity risk** – the risk that money has little potential for gain, depending on the interest rate

Even though money market funds are considered safer investments, it's important to know that a money market fund is actually a fund that seeks to preserve the value of the investment at $1 per share. Although it is rare, money market funds have dipped below $1 before. Many money markets are not insured by FDIC, so ask the bank how it is insured before investing in a money market.

What are the potential rewards?

Money is safe and available. It can also be insured by the FDIC, depending on the investment and the institution at which it is held. Although cash may or may not pay significant interest, it is a very important part of any portfolio. Cash allows an investor to maintain liquidity. If enough cash is on hand, it can prevent the need to sell investments at inopportune times. Cash on hand also allows an investor the opportunity to take advantage of market movement and buy when prices are low.

- MUTUAL FUND

    What is it?

    A mutual fund is an investment in which many people invest and a mutual fund manager buys stocks, bonds, commodities, or whatever the fund is allowed to buy. A mutual fund manager has some guidelines he or she must follow regarding investments that a particular mutual fund is allowed to purchase. An investor in a mutual fund owns a small piece of everything that the mutual fund owns. It is basically an investment pool that runs according to the specific objectives that are stated in that fund's prospectus (or summary of the mutual fund).

    How do they make money?

    Mutual funds make money when the value of the investments they hold goes up. They also make money when the investments pay interest or dividends.

    What are the potential risks?

    The primary risk of investing in mutual funds is that the value of the investments they hold goes down. Consequently, the value of the fund and each investor's share goes down. The specific risks are related to what the mutual fund companies invest in. Mutual funds are only bought or sold once a day--and for one amount. That amount is determined by the value of the investments the mutual fund companies hold at the end of the trading day. Another risk of mutual funds is that the investors share in the expenses and capital gains and losses of the fund as a whole, but they do not have control over the trading that produces these gains, losses or expenses. In essence, an investor can hold a fund and still be responsible for the decisions that other fund holders make.

    What are the potential rewards?

    Mutual funds are a way an investor can own pieces of a large number of investments for a relatively small amount of money. In some funds, investors are able to reap the rewards of a capital gain without investing a large portion of their money in one place. The funds are professionally managed. The fund managers buy and sell based on daily research and analysis. Mutual fund shares are easy to exchange, and there is often no charge for making an exchange. Be sure to read the fine print, though!

Some mutual funds also offer diversification within the funds, but it is important to note that not all do. An investor needs to be careful to choose the type of fund that fits his individual risk profile. We will go into that more in the asset allocation section.

• Exchange-Traded Fund

What is it?

Exchange-Traded Funds are investments that track the performance of a specific market index or group of securities that share a certain style, sector, country, or asset class. The investments represent a basket of securities that reflect the ETF goal and are not actively managed.

How can they make money?

Like mutual funds, ETFs make money when the investments within them increase in value.

What are the potential risks?

The main risk is that the value of the underlying investments decreases.

What are the potential rewards?

ETFs are able to be bought and sold on the market so an investor can buy or sell at any time of the trading day. They also have the potential for gains due to their relatively low cost of ownership. They are considered tax-efficient compared to mutual funds.

• Annuity

What is it?

An annuity is an investment that is covered by an insurance policy usually regarding the performance or the payment of the investment.

What is it used for?

Annuities are typically used to guarantee the safety of principal, or the security of the payout, or to achieve tax deferred growth. Annuities are categorized as fixed or variable. Fixed annuities have certain guarantees of return and/or payout based on the amount invested. Variable annuities are invested in funds specified by the issuing company and are guaranteed for a certain return or payout. Annuities can be covered by simple or complex guarantees, and they usually involve an investor committing to remain invested for at least a specified period of time. Annuity gains are also tax-deferred and can be an option for tax planning.

How can they make money?

Fixed annuities make money by growing at the rate agreed to in the contract, or by paying a fixed payment for a period of time. Variable annuities make money through either the contract agreement or through the increased value of the underlying investments.

What are the potential risks?

Annuities usually require that the investor commit to an investment of a certain minimum time period; therefore, they are typically not easily liquidated. The contractual obligations of the issuing company are included in the fees charged. These fees can decrease the investment return of the annuity.

What are the potential rewards?

Annuities can provide safety of principal and/or safety of an income stream. They also can be valuable estate-planning tools to pass on assets and/or guarantee a stream of income after someone dies. The growth of the value in annuities is tax-deferred and allows for tax-free reallocations of money. For long-term growth, tax deferral is often a good option. Death benefits of annuities also offer protection for heirs. Annuities and the laws surrounding them change often as new products are developed. Consult a tax advisor to understand the tax implications of an annuity.

EXERCISE: ARE YOU IN CONTROL, OR OVER-CONTROLLING?

To gain control over the parts of your life that are yours to dictate, you must know who you are. This exercise will help you find your own level of comfort with parts of your financial life. The illusion of control is one thing that can really 'get' you when you realize you don't have as much control as you thought. There are risks in life—both known and unknown. Your job is to plan for the known risks and to prepare so that the unknown risks will have not too large an impact.

> CONTROLLING THE CONTROLLABLE AND LETTING THE REST GO IS A KEY INGREDIENT TO MAINTAINING SANITY AND PERSPECTIVE WHEN INVESTING. YOU SHOULD ALSO BE AWARE OF HOW YOU TEND TO LOOK AT THINGS: DO YOU OVEREMPHASIZE THE GOOD WHILE IGNORING THE BAD, OR VICE VERSA?

1 – A FRIEND TELLS ME THAT THERE IS A GREAT INVESTMENT SHE KNOWS ABOUT. I:
__ FIND OUT HOW MUCH IT IS AND PLACE AN ORDER (1)
__ DO SOME RESEARCH ON THE WEB, FIND OUT A LITTLE, AND PLACE AN ORDER (2)
__ CAREFULLY AND THOROUGHLY STUDY THE INVESTMENT TO DECIDE WHETHER IT IS RIGHT FOR ME (3)

2 – MY COMPANY TELLS ME IT IS DOING GREAT, AND I KNOW I CAN INVEST IN IT IN MY RETIREMENT PLAN. I:
__ PUT ALL OF THE MONEY IN MY RETIREMENT PLAN INTO MY COMPANY'S STOCK; AFTER ALL, IT'S DOING WELL (1)
__ LOOK AT THE OTHER INVESTMENTS I HAVE BOTH IN AND OUT OF MY RETIREMENT PLAN AND DECIDE WHETHER MY COMPANY'S STOCK FITS (3)
__ EVALUATE WHAT I THINK OF MY COMPANY, THEN MAKE MY DECISION (2)
__ EVALUATE THE COMPANY'S FINANCIAL RECORDS AND ITS POTENTIAL, THEN LOOK AT MY INVESTMENTS AND SEE IF THE COMPANY FITS (3)

3 – My friends would say that I am...
___ ORGANIZED AND DO THINGS IN AN ORDERLY FASHION (3)
___ CRAZY AND UNPREDICTABLE, BUT FUN! (1)
___ A BIT OF A MESS, BUT I USUALLY GET THINGS DONE EVENTUALLY (2)

4 – If I invested 10% of my money into an investment that was supposed to go up, but it went down 50% for the first 6 months I owned it, I would
___ REEVALUATE THE INVESTMENT BY LOOKING AT THE INFORMATION AND WHAT WAS HAPPENING TO SIMILAR INVESTMENTS AND MAKE A DECISION (2)
___ CALL THE PERSON WHO SOLD IT TO ME; I'D BE DEVASTATED AND WOULD SELL (1)
___ EVALUATE THE MARKET AND MY GOALS FOR THE INVESTMENT AND DECIDE WHETHER THE INVESTMENT STILL FIT (3)

Add up your points. This is your control score.
- If you scored 1-4, you tend to be unpredictable and to act on a whim, not based on facts.
- If you scored 5-8, you are sort of unpredictable, but you think things through and check some facts.
- If you scored 9-12, you think before you leap and try to make decisions based on facts and control what you can.

Believe it or not, the ability to look at the potential for loss is a great thing when it comes to investing. Investing involves understanding what you can control, what you can't control, and the risks involved in any investment. For example, you can control the kind of investment you buy—and how much you buy. You can also control when you choose to sell. You can control how long you keep your investment. You can't control what the market is going to do between the time you buy and the time you sell.

You can control your research and your evaluation of an investment. You can't control whether your predictions come true.

Step 4 – Have a strategy for investing your money

Asset allocation is when money put into an investment portfolio is invested in different asset classes. An asset class is a category of investment. In other words, stocks of large companies are an asset class; bonds are another asset class.

A mix of investments may help balance risk and return. It can also help smooth out the returns of the portfolio in the long run. Asset allocation works because usually the forces or economic conditions that cause one type of investment to decline in value can cause another investment to rise.

Asset allocation is the idea that you can lessen your risk by strategically investing in certain areas of the market. Asset allocation can be considered for an entire portfolio, or to specific parts of a portfolio.

Asset allocation is the framework of an investment strategy. You might have several asset allocation plans. As you go through life, it is usually wise to continue to adjust your investment goals based on your needs.

Asset Allocation consists of separating investments into three major categories: Stocks, Bonds, and Cash. How you achieve this balance depends on what instruments are the most suitable for you. Some people prefer to own stock in specific companies; others like mutual funds that invest in stocks. With bonds, it is the same logic: some people like to own the bonds and some like to own the bond funds. If you are investing primarily through an employer retirement plan, the option is usually going to be mutual funds. Most retirement plans are only able to offer the stock of the company that sponsors the plan in those accounts.

According to research, over 90% of the results of long-term investing come from asset allocation, and 6% from being in the market at the proper time. Only 4% of long term investing success comes from picking the right investments.

In good times, people tend to want to take more risk than they may be able to handle, because the potential for loss seems less likely than it actually is. Similarly, in bad market times, people tend to overestimate the potential for further loss and underestimate the potential for gain. Through a disciplined investment strategy and asset allocation, people are more likely to remain on the path.

Diversification

Some investors believe that a strategy begins and ends with asset allocation. But asset allocation alone may not be enough to protect a portfolio and let the money do what it is supposed to. This is where we get to the idea of diversification.

What is diversification?

Diversification is spreading assets among different investments to reduce the portfolio's overall risk by taking many small risks instead of a few large ones. Diversification takes the pie that is formed in the asset allocation exercise and breaks it down into smaller chunks.

Diversification in an investment portfolio is the idea that an investor should balance investments. Stocks are divided in terms of sector, size, style, and country. With bonds, diversification is determined by maturity date, credit rating, issuer, and tax factors. Cash should be considered by your need for liquidity and the return that is available to you.

Diversification through different investment options potentially reduces risk, and it may bring even more consistent returns. But it doesn't ensure profit or loss.

Common misconceptions about diversification

- Multiple accounts or advisors means a portfolio is diversified.
  Not true. *An investor can have many investments and not be diversified.*
- Owning several mutual funds means a portfolio is diversified.
  Not necessarily true. *The amount of diversification depends on what those funds hold and how they work together.*
- A mix of stocks, bonds and cash means a portfolio is diversified.
  Not necessarily true. *It depends on what investments are held in each of those categories.*
- A diversified portfolio shelters an investor from all risk.
  Not true. *There are times where most asset classes decline in value.*

Pitfalls of improper diversification

- Taking too much risk for too little gain
- Not taking enough risk to get enough gain and therefore not building the wealth you need to achieve your goals
- Concentration in a stock or sector providing increased risk

What is Dollar Cost Averaging?

Dollar Cost Averaging is a way you can buy a little of an investment at a time to take advantage of the ups and downs of the market. The goal is to buy a lot when the investment is cheap and buy less when the investment is more expensive. Overall dollar cost averaging reduces the cost basis—or the amount paid—for the investment.

For example – you buy XYZ company stock one month and buy $100 worth of shares. The share price is $10, and you purchase 10 shares. If in the next month you buy $100 worth of shares and the share price is $20, you purchase 5 shares. You now own a total of 15 shares and have bought them for a total of $200, so the average price per share is $13.33. If the following month you buy an additional $100 and the shares now cost $25 a share, you get 4 shares. You now own 19 shares and have spent $300. Even though the last shares you bought were for $25 a share, the average cost per share was $15.78.

When you invest mutual funds or stock through an employer plan you usually engage in dollar cost averaging. A portion of your paycheck goes into your account and is invested in the funds you choose, Since this happens on a regular basis you are dollar cost averaging.

Re-balancing

An important thing to consider for your portfolio is periodic re-balancing, something you should do on a regular schedule. When you re-balance your portfolio, you return the asset allocation to your originally intended allocation. Investment vehicles gain and lose value at different rates, and they can get out of balance. Even if they are all gaining value, some segments will always be gaining faster than others. When you re-balance your portfolio, you sell some of the investments that are over their stated allocations and buy some that are under their stated allocation to achieve the original balance. This keeps your level of risk constant.

STEP 5 – PATIENCE PAYS OFF

Have you ever started an exercise or study routine? Are you still following the first exercise routine you ever started? Are you following the second one, the third one? Do you still need to find one that works?

Much like exercising or studying, investing requires discipline, dedication, and patience. Also like exercising, it can be incredibly fun and rewarding--or dull and boring. It's up to you: much of your investment work involves creating a system that works for *you*. That's why professionals may or may not play a role in your investing life.

To achieve the long-term results that you set forth in your plan, you have to have some discipline. Often, this means holding your emotions at bay. Even the best investors give in to their emotions at some point, but with discipline, they are much less likely to incur big losses based on short-sighted investment decisions. Our emotions often tell us to do exactly the opposite of what we know we need to do; it feels better to put money in when the world is good and the market has gone up for a long while. And putting money in at the bottom is scary, because the world often seems as if it is going to end. Discipline will help you put money in and take money out at what may seem like the most difficult times.

Investing is a long-term activity that requires you to be committed and patient. The movement of the market can play with your hopes and dreams for the future. Investors with solid plans and the discipline to stick to their plans have a higher likelihood of achieving their stated goals than those who invest without plans.

Staying on Track

Do
- Have a plan for all investments
- Monitor the investment performance quarterly, and rebalance annually
- Consider how each investment change affects the overall portfolio
- Invest wisely based on facts
- Remember, this is a marathon, not a sprint

Do Not
- Look at accounts daily or weekly
- Make changes to the asset allocation without understanding how the changes impact the portfolio's asset allocation
- Make large bets in any "hot" area of the market
- Invest based on hunches, tips from others or emotions
- Invest in products that do not meet stated goals or objectives

Risky Business

When things are going poorly in the investment markets, you hear a lot about risk--the risk of this investment, the risk of the market going down, the risk that inflation will make your investment worth less. When things are going well in the markets, there is little talk about risk and a lot of talk about how much money everyone is making, and how much money there is to be made. The risk of an investment or a group of investments is almost always underrated until it's too late.

There are numerous theories on how to time the market and how to go against popular thinking. Over time, as an investor, you will develop some theories on your own or with your advisors. No matter how much someone tells you they know what is going to happen, they don't know, and neither do you. Theories are fine; facts are better.

In investing, fear is good. Fear means that you have looked at the risk, you have evaluated it, and you've made a decision. A dose of fear means that you are well aware of the potential for loss. If you have fear and still choose to purchase an investment, it's because you decided that the potential for gain outweighs the potential for loss. If you don't have any fear, you'd better look at the potential for loss again.

The amount of risk you take in investing is not always the same as the amount you're willing to take in other parts of your life. It takes time to get to know this part of yourself. You may like to cliff-dive, but you may be petrified of losing any amount of money. On the other hand, you may be a person who only drives well under the speed limit, but has no problem buying a risky investment.

In the end, it's *your* money and *your* goals that are on the line--not those of your advisors, or of the person on the other end of the phone or online chat. It is not your best friend's money or your mother or father's. It is *your's*, so your own risk level (and that of your spouse) is the only one you need to consider.

Your Tolerance for Risk

So... How risky are you? There is no right or wrong answer here, and there's no scoring in this exercise. It's simply intended to help you get to know yourself—and your tolerance for risk— a little better.

1. If I made an investment that I was told had the potential to go up or down 10% in a year and it went down 5% in the first 6 months, I would...

   _____

   And I would feel _____

   Because _____

2. If I kept all of my money in cash and the stock market went up 20% in a year, I would...

   _____

   And I would feel _____

   Because _____

3. If I took a friend's tip and bought stock in a company that I did not know anything about, and the stock gained 40% in 2 days, I would...

   _____

   And I would feel _____

   Because _____

4. IF I BOUGHT THE SAME STOCK AND IT INSTEAD WENT DOWN 40% IN ONE DAY, I WOULD...

_____

AND I WOULD FEEL _____

BECAUSE _____

LOOK AT YOUR LAST TWO ANSWERS. WHICH DO YOU FEEL MORE STRONGLY?
DOES IT FEEL MORE REAL TO THINK OF THE GAIN OR THE LOSS?

5. IF I BOUGHT AN INVESTMENT, AND IN THE FIRST YEAR IT WENT UP 10%, THE NEXT YEAR IT WENT DOWN 10% AND THE NEXT YEAR IT WENT UP 15%, I WOULD...

_____

AND I WOULD FEEL _____

BECAUSE _____

6. IF I BOUGHT AN INVESTMENT, AND IN THE FIRST YEAR IT WENT UP 45%, THE NEXT YEAR IT WENT DOWN 20% AND THE NEXT YEAR IT WENT DOWN 2%, I WOULD...

_____

AND I WOULD FEEL _____

BECAUSE _____

NOW LOOK AT THE LAST TWO SCENARIOS. THE REALITY IS THAT IN EACH OF THESE CASES, YOU END UP WITH ALMOST THE EXACT SAME AMOUNT OF MONEY.
HOW DO YOU FEEL ABOUT EACH SCENARIO?
DO YOU FEEL THE SAME OR DIFFERENTLY ABOUT THEM? WHY?

INVESTING NEWS — WHAT'S IN THE MEDIA

To understand even a fraction of what you see in the news, you have to know the lingo and know how to use it. There is an entire segment of the media dedicated to covering the latest news in investing. There is a barrage of information that we can't even be sure is understood by the people covering the news. Although it may be fun to listen to, and you may get some knowledge from it, remember that broadcast media outlets are mostly selling entertainment. People who go on TV or the Internet or radio and tell you to do something do not know you. You and the professionals or people that you trust are the only ones who know your situation. You have to interpret what the media say and decide if any of it applies to *you*.

The more you know your goals and are confident in your strategy, the less likely you are to make rash changes based on what you hear on TV. And it's helpful to remember that whether an event is good or bad for you depends on your perspective and on your personal situation. A steep drop in the market may be very bad for someone who is invested and needs to use that money soon; yet it can be very good for someone who has money to invest and can hold on long enough for the market to cycle back up.

There are some terms and tools that you should know about when listening to the media:

INDEXES

An index is a measure that is intended to be indicative of something larger. Listed below are the most common stock indexes and what they track.

Standard and Poor's 500 – Commonly known as the S&P 500. This index tracks the prices of the 500 largest stocks actively traded in the US.

Dow Jones Industrial Average – or the Dow – The Dow is a complex calculation of the stock prices of 30 companies chosen by the editors of the Wall Street Journal. These companies are not necessarily industrial in nature as the name would suggest. The components are occasionally changed, and they represent large U.S. institutions.

NASDAQ – or the National Association of Securities Dealers Automated Quote – The NASDAQ is not an index at all; it's a trading system that is often treated like an index. The NASDAQ is an automated quoting system on which the stocks of technology companies are traded.

MSCI EAFE – The Morgan Stanley Capital International East, Australiasia and Far East Index - The MSCI EAFE is an index of foreign stocks, those in about 21 countries excluding the US and Canada.

Stocks can also be categorized by the sectors or industries in which they do business. There are 10 sectors used by investors:
-Consumer Discretionary
-Consumer Staples
-Energy
-Financials
-Healthcare
-Industrials
-Information Technology
-Materials
-Telecommunication
-Utilities

These sectors are defined by the Global Industry Classification Standard.

Although there are countless other indexes, these are the ones usually quoted most on the nightly news. They do provide indicators, but it's debatable what those indicators really tell investors. In the case of the Dow, it's arguable that the daily performance of 30 companies is a slim sample of the thousands of companies whose stocks are traded daily.

Benchmarking

A **benchmark** is a point of reference that is supposed to allow you to evaluate the performance of something. In investing, this is when you compare your portfolio to one or a combination of the indexes.

A word on benchmarking: it can be helpful, but it can also be a bit like comparing yourself to your neighbor. You have to know what your objectives are, and those of the benchmark, to determine if you are comparing apples to apples. If your portfolio is heavy in large U.S. stocks, the S&P 500 might be an appropriate indicator of how your portfolio is doing relative to the rest. The most important thing is how you are tracking against your goals--not how you are doing relative to the market. It can be tempting to feel good or bad based on what the market is doing, but in the end, if your money is not there to work for you, then your goals will not be met. A strong focus on goals and a steady path will go a long way to achieving those goals.

Other Terms to know:

Bear Market –A period of declining value in a market

Bull Market – A period of rising value in a market

Total Return – The rate of return of an investment including all dividends and interest. This includes the change in the value of the investment.

Volatility – The tendency of an investment to experience fluctuation in value over the short term

Know about the Tax Man

In order to be an informed investor, you must know the basics of how your money is taxed--both when you earn it and when you invest it. As you build up your savings, a good tax strategy and a great tax advisor will be valuable for you to have. Taxes are a very important part of investing.

To understand when and how taxes are levied on investments, you have to think about how investments make money. They make money in a few simple ways:

- An investment is worth more when you sell it than when you bought it
- An investment pays you a dividend
- An investment pays you interest

Taxable vs. Tax-Deferred Accumulation

Understanding and limiting tax exposure when possible is one way to help your portfolio meet financial goals.

In a taxable account, you pay taxes on any money that you earn from your investments as that money is earned. But you are free to withdraw money from the account for any reason, and you do not have to pay taxes on that withdrawal.

In a tax-deferred account, you do not pay any taxes on the money that you earn as you earn it. When you sell investments or receive interest or dividend income, that money is not taxed. And depending on the type of account and the benefits of that account, you may or may not have to pay taxes when you withdraw the money.

7

LEGAL LESSONS FOR LIFE

The law can be intimidating. This can be especially true when you don't really know how—and when-- it applies to you. In this chapter, we'll explore the side of the law that is all about protecting yourself and the people that you love. We will also discuss issues you'll need to consider, and actions you must take in your legal life.

YOU'RE OVER 18. DID YOU KNOW.....

DECIDING WHO HAS THE POWER

WHERE THERE'S A WILL, THERE'S A WAY

WHAT DID YOU DO—OR WHAT ARE YOU PLANNING TO DO—AT 18? REGISTER TO VOTE? HAVE A PARTY? CELEBRATE?

YOU'RE OVER 18. DID YOU KNOW...

To many teens, turning 18 simply means that they gain independence. But you also gain a great deal of responsibility. Most importantly, it means that your parents or guardians are no longer legally responsible for you, as they were when you were a minor. What this really means to you is that those things that your parents could do for you easily (i.e. signing a lease or acting as your medical advocate) might not be so easy anymore.

You may be thinking, *'I don't have anything or anyone that depends on me; therefore, I have no legal needs.'* Not so fast. There are certain legal documents that are necessary for *everyone* over the age of 18.

Imagine this: It's the day after your 18th birthday. You're in an accident and are unconscious. Your mom, dad, or former guardian comes to the hospital to see you and to talk to the doctors. The doctor tells them that she is sorry, but she can't talk to them because there is no document from you that says she can discuss your condition. Would a doctor do this? Maybe or maybe not. She doesn't know whether you would want her to talk with your mom, dad, or guardian. But if she has the proper document, she can tell them everything they need to know and she can rely on them to help make important medical decisions on your behalf while you are incapacitated. Do you want to take the chance that the doctor won't talk to your loved ones? If not, read on.

DECIDING WHO HAS THE POWER

There are three critical documents of Estate Planning for anyone over 18:
- A Durable Financial Power of Attorney
- A Healthcare Power of Attorney, or Living Will
- A Will

Please note that wills and estate planning issues are controlled by the state in which you live. Each state has different laws and specific documentation required. Each state deals with personal property differently and has specific documents to protect you and your family.

Definitions

Durable Financial Power of Attorney – A Durable Financial Power of Attorney allows you to appoint someone to make financial decisions and to assist with personal responsibilities. There are several types of Powers of Attorney available. One of the critical differences in Powers of Attorney is when and how the agent can make decisions for you. Many people choose a parent or a spouse to do this job. The person you choose must act in your best interests, maintain accurate records, keep property separate from their personal property, and avoid any conflict of interest.

Healthcare Power of Attorney and/or Living Will - A Healthcare Power of Attorney and/or a Living Will is a document that states your beliefs and wishes with regard to your healthcare if you are not able to make decisions and communicate. This document names the person or people who are legally appointed to make medical decisions. This critical document will allow for ease of decision-making as well as a way to make sure your moral beliefs are honored.

We'll talk more about each type of Power of Attorney, including why it's important, and whom you should consider for each responsibility. It's important for you to pick people who are in your life for the long term. They have the potential to have a lot of power in your life, so make sure to pick someone whom you fully trust.

What does it mean to allow someone to act on your behalf? The person to whom you grant your power of attorney can make decisions as if she were you. Anything that you give her the power to do, she can do. If you give her power of attorney over your brokerage account, she can buy and sell stocks, bonds, or whatever she wants to, in your account. You must be careful whom you choose--and be careful about what power you give that person. You also have to be specific about when he/she is to get that power.

Durable Financial Powers of Attorney

When you're in charge of your own finances, you don't have to do anything to make sure that your finances are taken care of--other than being accountable and following the guidelines in this book. But what happens if you're suddenly unable to take care of your financial world?

A Durable Financial Power of Attorney allows you to appoint someone you trust to assist with financial decisions. This same person you appoint can sign documents for you and bind you to the decisions they make on your behalf. There are several types of Durable Powers of Attorney, but there are two main types used in most states. One of the critical differences in Durable Powers of Attorney is determined by when the appointed person can take action. When can he or she begin to make decisions for you? The person you appoint as your durable power of attorney is called your **agent**.

THINK ABOUT IT: HOW WOULD YOU WANT SOMEONE TO HANDLE YOUR MONEY FOR 1 MINUTE, 1 WEEK, 1 MONTH, 1 YEAR, OR FOREVER?

_____

_____

WOULD YOU LIKE FOR THEM TO DO NOTHING? DO A LOT?

_____

_____

WOULD YOU LIKE FOR THEM TO BE ABLE TO INQUIRE ABOUT YOUR BENEFITS? YOUR HEALTH INSURANCE?

_____

_____

WOULD YOU LIKE FOR THEM TO BE ABLE TO TALK WITH YOUR LANDLORD OR MORTGAGE COMPANY? OR TALK WITH YOUR CREDIT CARD COMPANY?

_____

_____

WOULD YOU LIKE FOR THEM TO BE ABLE TO COMMUNICATE WITH YOUR EMPLOYER ON YOUR BEHALF?

_____

_____

WOULD YOU LIKE FOR THEM TO BE ABLE TO MAKE DEPOSITS OR TRANSFERS OR HANDLE ANY ISSUES IN YOUR ACCOUNTS?

_____

_____

WHO IN YOUR FAMILY OR TRUSTED CIRCLE OF FRIENDS WOULD HANDLE YOUR MONEY AND FINANCES THE WAY YOU HAVE DESCRIBED ABOVE?

_____

_____

REMEMBER THAT SOONER OR LATER, YOU'LL MOST LIKELY BE ABLE TO RESUME CONTROL OF YOUR FINANCES, SO MAKE SURE YOU SELECT AN AGENT WHO WILL HANDLE THEM WELL WHILE YOU CANNOT.

The Job Description

One thing to consider when choosing whom to appoint as your agent is his skill set. Does the job description fit his skill set?

Taking a look at the rights and duties of an agent of the Durable Power of Attorney can give you an idea of the skill sets required. These tasks are listed in the forms supplied by the state in which you live. The rights given to your chosen agent can be very broad, but you can give your agent as much or as little power as you wish. You may want to give your agent authority to do some or all of the following:

Authority of a Durable Financial Power of Attorney

The person you list as your financial power of attorney has the legal authority to act on your behalf. You can specify which transactions he can perform. You can also exclude any specific transaction. What this means is that the powers can be chosen individually or an agent can be given broad powers to cover all areas.

Examples:
- Use assets to pay your everyday expenses and those of your family
- Buy, sell, maintain, pay taxes, and mortgage your real estate and other property
- Handle your benefits from Social Security, Medicare, Medicaid, or other governmental programs, or military service; manage any issues regarding these governmental agencies
- Buy, sell, maintain, and pay taxes on stocks, bonds, mutual funds, commodity and options transactions
- Handle your transactions with banks and other financial institutions
- Handle any transactions with regard to your 401K and other retirement plans
- Handle your tax matters
- Buy and sell your insurance policies and annuities
- File and pay your taxes
- Operate your business or handle day-to-day operations of your business
- Claim property you inherited or are otherwise entitled to
- Transfer property to a trust that you previously created
- Manage any legal claims pending or litigation
- Manage your property
- Act on your behalf with third parties
- Handle any of your estate, trust, and other beneficiary transactions

Decisions to make in a Durable Financial Power of Attorney: The challenging decision is *when* the absolute power should be granted. We say "absolute power" because the person you choose has the right to transact legally binding business on your behalf.

- A Durable Financial Power of Attorney can take effect from the date signed, meaning the date the document is signed. The person you choose can go out and transact business for you, even if you are still able to act on your own behalf. Many couples have a clause in their Durable Financial Power of Attorney so that one can transact business for the other on an everyday basis. For example, if there is a checking account in your name, your agent can write a check that day on your account. Be VERY careful about giving anyone this right.
- A Durable Financial Power of Attorney can also become effective upon incapacity. This can require a doctor's certification to become effective. The person you choose cannot transact business, such as getting money from the bank, unless you are incapacitated and your condition is verified.

If you download any of these documents from the Internet or copy a document, know which type of Durable Financial Power Attorney you're signing. There are a few states that require the Durable Financial Power of Attorney to be recorded with the county in which the signor lives to make them valid. Check the laws in your county.

How to choose a financial agent:
  - Think about the exercise you did in this chapter. How do you want your money to be handled? Here are some good things to consider:
  - Does this person handle money wisely? What is her financial situation?
  - Look at the powers given to this person and consider his skill set.
  - Is she a trusted family member or best friend who is good with money? Does he pay his bills on time? Is she strapped for money?
  - The person you choose as financial agent might have different skills than a healthcare power of attorney.
  - This person does not have to be family member; the key is to choose someone you trust. Who else might you appoint as your financial agent in case the primary person is not able to fulfill the duties? Consider more than one person.

Things to remember about a Durable Financial Power of Attorney:
- Know which type of document is being signed, or when the power to act on your behalf begins.
- Know which type is appropriate for a particular situation.

- Each state uses a different form, and many financial companies have their own customized forms that they want to have signed in addition to a Durable Financial Power of Attorney. The financial company may not require its specific customized documents, but it does make it easier and quicker to use the specified form. If you do not use their customized forms, they may require legal review by their in-house counsel and there may be a delay in the right to use it and act as an agent.
- You may give your agent the right to perform specific actions but withhold the right to perform others.
- Durable Financial Powers of Attorney generally require both witnesses and notaries. It is wise to have at least 2 witnesses--even if the state requirement is only one witness.

Ways of discontinuing a Durable Financial Power of Attorney:

Death. A Durable Power of Attorney automatically ends if you die. The person you chose as your Financial Power of Attorney does not have authority to handle things after your death, such as paying debts, making funeral or burial arrangements, or transferring property to the people who inherit it. The person in charge upon death is the Executor of the Will.

Cancellation. As long as you are mentally competent, a Durable Power of Attorney can be revoked at any time.

Divorce. In some states, if your spouse is an agent and you get a divorce, your spouse's authority is automatically terminated. In other states, to end an ex-spouse's authority, you have to revoke an existing Durable Financial Power of Attorney. It is wise to make a new document as separation is anticipated or divorce is filed.

Court invalidation. It is rare, but a court may declare the document invalid if it concludes that you were not mentally competent when the document was signed--or that you were the victim of fraud or undue influence.

Unavailable agent. To avoid this problem, name an alternate in the document.

Abuses of Durable Financial Powers of Attorney:

Unfortunately, the potential for fraud is great. Unlawful gifting and embezzlement are common. Sometimes agents deplete the majority of the signor's estate, open bank accounts with new titles, or change beneficiary designations. If the agent has abused his or her powers, you should have grounds to sue for return of property and assets and monetary damages. If the abuse is uncovered by beneficiaries after the signor has died, they may be able to sue for a number of causes of action. It is unlikely that all the money that was taken illegally will be returned, so it's very important to protect yourself by choosing the right agent. Use your head--not your heart. Let's revisit the exercise above and see if the answer is the same.

exercise

When would you like for someone to have these powers? You can choose for this person's powers to take effect either from the date you sign the paper or in the event that you are incapacitated or otherwise unable to perform these duties, as certified by a doctor.

The power they will have	From the date you sign the Power of Attorney	If you are incapacitated
Pay your everyday expenses and those of your family		
Buy, sell, maintain, pay taxes on, and mortgage real estate and other property		
Handle benefits from Social Security, Medicare, Medicaid, or other governmental programs, or military service. Manage any issues regarding these governmental agencies.		
Buy, sell, maintain, and pay taxes on stocks, bonds, mutual funds, commodity and options transactions		
Handle transactions with banks and other financial institutions		
Handle any transactions with regard to your 401K and other retirement plans		
Buy and sell insurance policies		
File and pay your taxes		
Operate your business: handle day-to-day operations of the business		
Claim property you have inherited or are otherwise entitled to		
Manage property by acting on your behalf		
Claims and litigation: To manage any pending legal claims or litigation		

This may sound like a lot, but it's extremely important to know what power you are giving someone and why you are giving it.

> WHO IN YOUR FAMILY OR TRUSTED CIRCLE OF FRIENDS WOULD WISELY HANDLE YOUR MONEY AND FINANCES? WOULD HE OR SHE BE ABLE TO DO ANY OR ALL OF THE TASKS DESCRIBED ABOVE?

HEALTHCARE POWER OF ATTORNEY AND/OR A LIVING WILL

A Healthcare Power of Attorney is similar to a Durable Financial Power of Attorney. The difference is that the power given in this document applies only to healthcare decisions. Your Healthcare Power of Attorney appoints someone to make healthcare decisions if you are not able to do so.

Depending on the state, the Healthcare Power of Attorney can be a separate document from a Living Will, or they can be incorporated into one document. Many states keep the most updated documents online and available, usually at no cost. Check out your state's website or consult an attorney to see which is most common in your state. Normally, the correct state form can be downloaded from the Internet.

REASONS TO HAVE A HEALTHCARE POWER OF ATTORNEY NOW:
- Medical decisions may need to be made quickly.
- Court proceedings to appoint a Healthcare Power of Attorney will take time even if a quick hearing is requested. There will be attorney and court involvement, and there may even be a disagreement as to who should be appointed.
- Choosing a person who knows your wishes allows the medical team to focus on healthcare. Otherwise, they will be wasting valuable time in determining who is the legally correct person with the right to make those decisions for you.

DECISIONS TO MAKE IN A HEALTHCARE POWER OF ATTORNEY:
  - Carefully read and make sure you understand what options are given in the document.
  - Think about your wishes and who best can carry them out.
  - Have conversations with trusted people, including what they would be able to do in terms of life-prolonging procedures. Would they be able to follow your moral or ethical wishes?
  - The analysis of what you want, and frank discussions with those trusted people, are just as critical as filling out the piece of paper.

WHEN CHOOSING A HEALTHCARE AGENT:
- She must be able to speak effectively with healthcare practitioners and be a strong advocate for you.
- He should be guided by your preferences—even if they are different from his own personal beliefs.
- Your agent must be willing to act in this role.
- Choose more than one agent, as they will need to be available quickly in many circumstances.
- Choose someone who can emotionally handle emergency situations.
- Consider an agent who lives nearby, or a co-agent who can be available and arrive quickly.
- Examples of issues for consideration and discussion include the following:
    - Whether you want life prolonging treatment if you enter into a comatose state or irreversible condition;
    - Whether you want food and water fed through a tube; and
    - Whether you want to grant permission to the Healthcare Power of Attorney to have a feeding tube removed.

It will all depend on the state-approved document as to what is considered. You should put your specific wishes or instructions in writing.

Now let's review these critical steps. You need to carefully read what you are signing and fully understand what options are given in the documents. You need to think about what your wishes are and who best can carry out those wishes. Have conversations with those trusted family members, including what you would want in terms of life-prolonging procedures.

If you would choose to have every medical procedure done that could possibly lead to recovery, it's not smart to choose someone whose belief system supports only the relief of pain in life-threatening situations. Could this person set aside her own beliefs to allow you to get the care that you desire?

HIPAA Law (Health Insurance Portability and Accountability Act) details:
Healthcare Powers of Attorney become more and more critical for any person over 18 years old. When a child turns 18, the parent technically has no legal right to make medical decisions for their child without a Healthcare Power of Attorney.

As part of the big 18th birthday event, have the Healthcare Power of Attorney ready to be signed! It is a simple gift for the whole family.

Healthcare Power of Attorney is critical when a minor child is living with step-parents or with a person who is not their biological parent. The document is simple to draw up and makes medical emergencies easier.

Steps to obtaining and maintaining a Healthcare Power of Attorney:
Each form will need to be signed *and* witnessed (not by a family member or the agent).

Give one copy to the primary doctor, one to the decision maker, and one to those family or friends who would likely be called in an emergency.

Keep a card in your wallet or purse stating that a Healthcare Power of Attorney has been written and where it can be found. Some states have an online filing system to register Healthcare Powers of Attorney

Review the Healthcare Power of Attorney from time to time and change it if necessary. When, or if, admitted as a patient to a hospital or health care agency, always bring a copy of the Healthcare Power or Attorney and give a copy to a member of the hospital staff to be placed in the medical record. This must be presented each time you are admitted to the hospital.

A Living Will is a statement about treatment philosophy so that the physicians can understand your wishes. The living will cannot handle all potential decisions a healthcare agent might confront, but it can be a good road map. Many states combine the Living Will and the Healthcare Power of Attorney into one document.

Limitations of Living Wills:
They address only a narrow range of end-of-life decisions
They cannot cover all the serious medical circumstances a person may face

A Living Will can provide general guidance to healthcare practitioners and your substitute decision-makers in the face of serious illness.

WHO CAN HANDLE THE POWER?

Deciding who should have the power to stand in and make decisions for you is difficult. One of the best ways to make this critical choice is to think about the strengths of the people who are close to you. Just because you love someone or think he is strong in one area does not mean he's adept at everything. Some people perform well under pressure or when large tasks are in their hands, while other people don't. We are going to walk through figuring out who the right people are for the job.

Remember, you will want to list more than one person as your Healthcare Power or Attorney, in case the first person cannot be reached. Answer the questions below by listing the people you trust who would do well at these tasks.

WHO WOULD BE GOOD AT TALKING WITH DOCTORS AND MAKING DECISIONS?

_____

_____

WHO WOULD BE ABLE TO FOLLOW THE DIRECTION YOU HAVE IN WRITING ABOUT WHAT YOU WANT?

_____

_____

WHOM ARE YOU ABLE TO HAVE A CONVERSATION WITH NOW ABOUT WHAT YOU WOULD WANT IF THEY HAD TO CHOOSE WHETHER TO PROLONG YOUR LIFE?

_____

_____

WHOSE BELIEFS ARE ALIGNED WITH YOURS? OR WHO COULD ADHERE TO YOUR BELIEFS EVEN IF HIS/HERS WERE DIFFERENT?

_____

_____

WHOM WOULD YOU TRUST TO MAKE DECISIONS FOR YOU?

_____

_____

WHO HAS A LEVEL HEAD IN EMERGENCY SITUATIONS?

_____

_____

WHO WOULD BE WILLING TO ACT AS AN ADVOCATE FOR YOU?

_____

_____

Where There's a Will, There's a Way

The final document you need is a will. It's often the case that as a young adult, you carry a feeling of invincibility—the sense that you're going to 'live forever'. That carries with it a lack of concern for long-term planning—especially when it comes to your life. A will is usually the last thing on your mind, but it should be one of the first things you consider when you become an independent adult.

By writing a will, you are making critical decisions for what should happen in the event of your death. Who will inherit your assets? Who will be the guardian of your minor children? No one wants to think about death. It is a sad and scary thing to consider. But the reality is that we all die at some point-- hopefully later rather than sooner. So take control. Don't leave these decisions about your money, your possessions, and your children up to a judge.

Try thinking about writing a will as a continued way for you to take care of your family. Since you won't be there to take care of them, you can make it easier for them to function as a family unit if you have this document in place.

Also, please be aware that confusion, grief, and the possibility of inheriting money can bring out the worst in the people you leave behind. Conflict can be overwhelming--on top of grief. Communication is the key to helping people get through.

The generic term 'will' covers a range of documents, from a simple will to a very complicated document dealing with complex issues. You have a range of choices for how to prepare your will. You can do it online, go to a will preparation service, or consult an Estate Planning Attorney who can handle a complex estate.

Please be cautious. If you aren't comfortable with analyzing the details and the implications of the downloaded will, find a flat- fee attorney who can handle the process for you.

If you read through the will that you downloaded and don't understand what the legal terms mean, *do not sign it*. It is critical that you fully understand any legal document you sign.

In law, the use of a single word or a single "term of art" can change the meaning of the document and change a legal interpretation. It is critical to see an attorney for some of the more complex legal documents or if you are unsure about anything in the will.

A will may be simple, but it can cover a lot

A will is a legal document that affirms the wishes of a person and their plans for dependents and for possessions. Wills vary greatly, but generally include naming an executor, guardianship of dependents, and transfer of property. In the absence of a will, the future of dependents and property is decided by the court.

We will explain and simplify some critical positions of trust that need to be appointed in a will. Next, we will discuss which documents require them. More importantly, the skills and qualities needed for each position will be detailed. In essence, we will give you the job description of each and what skills are needed to fill the job.

Guardian

- A guardian is usually appointed in a will for a minor child.
- A guardian is usually appointed in a will for an adult child who cannot take care of himself or herself. Often this adult child may have a disability.
- A guardian can also be appointed for an adult declared incompetent by the court in an action called guardianship. This occurs when the adult is no longer able to take care of herself, either financially or physically, and no prior planning has been done.
- A guardian can be anyone over the age of 18. The position includes the following duties:
  Powers and responsibilities similar to a parent.
  Making personal decisions for the ward such as living arrangements, education, social activities, and authorizing or withholding of medical or other professional care, treatment, or advice (when included in letters appointing guardian).

Often an adult child is appointed guardian for a senior citizen. Many times the decline is gradual, and it's difficult to actually make the decision that guardianship is necessary. The guardian will take care of the person who has difficulty in taking care of himself.

Strengths needed to be a guardian to a child:
- Compassion
- Stable family home
- Ability to treat the child like their own
- Similar moral values to those of the parent
- Patience and love
- Physical health to take on the parent role

Legal Lessons for Life

Strengths needed to be a guardian to a senior or an incompetent adult:
- Patience and love
- Physical health to take on the parent role
- Time and willingness to understand complex issues
- Living near the incompetent adult if they live on their own or the ability to bring the loved one into their home

Even if you don't want to complete this exercise because you don't have kids or an adult for whom you are guardian, go through it anyway. You may become a guardian some day, so know what it involves.

WHO IN YOUR FAMILY OR TRUSTED CIRCLE HAS THESE TRAITS?

COMPASSION

_____

A STABLE FAMILY HOME

_____

THE ABILITY TO TREAT THE CHILD LIKE THEIR OWN

_____

SIMILAR MORAL VALUES IN RAISING THE CHILD

_____

PATIENCE AND LOVE

_____

PHYSICAL HEALTH TO TAKE ON THE PARENT ROLE

_____

THE WILL TO TAKE CARE OF THE CHILD

_____

Executor

An executor is chosen to carry out the wishes and instructions in a will. This person will handle contact with an attorney and make decisions consistent with the details of the Will that was written by the deceased. He or she will be the point of contact for the beneficiaries. An executor can also be appointed by the court if no will has been found or executed.

Strengths needed to be an Executor:
- Ability to deal with paperwork and deadlines
- Ability to hire and work with attorneys
- Ability to have relationships with beneficiaries
- A peacemaker during stressful times

WHO IN YOUR FAMILY OR TRUSTED CIRCLE HAS THESE TRAITS?

DETAIL-ORIENTED WITH PAPERWORK

_____

PEACEMAKER DURING STRESSFUL TIMES

_____

ABILITY TO WORK WITH FAMILY MEMBERS WHO MAY NOT AGREE

_____

COMFORTABLE HIRING AND WORKING WITH ATTORNEYS

_____

ABLE TO MEET DEADLINES

_____

LEVEL-HEADED UNDER STRESS

_____

Trustee

A trustee is appointed to take care of property and finances for a minor child, or a trust set up to pay out on behalf of a beneficiary. This can be an individual or corporation.

Similar to a trustee, a conservator is appointed by the court to manage funds and finances of an individual not able to take care of that function. This can be an individual or corporation.

A trustee or a conservator has the powers and responsibilities of a fiduciary and is held to the standard of care of a prudent person dealing with someone else's property. This differs from a guardian in that the trustee or conservator does not decide where the person in need of assistance lives. The trustee ensures that the bills are paid and property is preserved.

Strengths needed to be a trustee or conservator
- Good manager
- Ability to understand basic investment concepts
- Ability to manage funds or hire a good investment advisor
- Ability to manage record keeping
- Ability to discern what is a monetary 'want' and what is a 'need'
- Discretion

WHO IN YOUR FAMILY OR TRUSTED CIRCLE HAS THESE TRAITS?

AN EFFECTIVE MANAGER

_____

KNOWLEDGE OF OR WILLINGNESS TO LEARN ABOUT INVESTMENTS

_____

COMFORT WORKING WITH PROFESSIONALS

_____

ACCURACY IN RECORD KEEPING

_____

KNOWLEDGE OF TAX RECORDS OR ABILITY TO WORK WITH THE CPAS WHO HANDLE THEM

_____

ABILITY TO KEEP THINGS TO THEMSELVES

_____

Without a will...

The courts are left to decide what happens to dependents, possessions and money you leave behind.

One Simple Example of Lack of a Will and some surprising results:

Dying 'intestate' means dying without a will. If you die without a will, the state will decide who gets your money and your property. If you're single, your assets will generally go to your parents or your siblings, or some combination of both.

Some married people assume that they do not need a will because all of the estate would go to their spouse. Generally, if a person dies without a will, the estate is left to that person's closest relatives. The state determines who that is by statute.

If you think you don't need a will because your spouse is entitled to inherit your whole estate, you may be mistaken. If you are married, a spouse is the likely person to receive a portion of the funds.

Here's an example from one specific U.S. state of what would happen to an estate when there is no will. This state includes surviving parents, but no tbrothers or sisters. It does not take into consideration pending divorces that are not final.

Married and Dying Intestate

	Real Property	Personal Property
Spouse and 1 Child	Spouse 50% Child 50%	$30,000 or less- Spouse 100% $30,000 or more- Spouse 50% Child 50%
Spouse and 2 or more children	Spouse 33 1/3% Children 66 2/3%	$30,000 or less- Spouse 100% $30,000 or more- Spouse 33 1/3% Child 66 2/3%
Spouse with no children and a surviving parent	Spouse 50% Parent 50%	$50,000 or less- Spouse 100% $50,000 or more- Spouse 50% Parent 50%
Spouse Only	Spouse 100%	Spouse 100%

Surprised that the surviving parent will inherit in this particular state? Other states have different inheritance structures if a person dies intestate. Don't make any assumptions; get it together and make a will!

Epilogue

Congratulations! You have achieved the first feat in taking control of your personal financial and legal life. By assuming an active, deliberate role in your financial future, you have already taken a big step in the right direction.

You've started your financial and legal education by building the foundation. As you grow and change and learn more about your needs as an independent person, *Get It Together* will provide a variety of resources to guide you through life. Keep this book as an ongoing resource, and look for other titles from *Get It Together* as you navigate life's many challenges and changes.

We have covered everything from savings accounts to insurance and wills. Still, this is just the beginning of your lifetime of learning. Financial products and services are constantly changing. We hope you'll keep up with what's going on by following along with us over the years. The more you know, the better you'll feel about the decisions you make. And you'll be better prepared for those inevitable rainy days.

You have also learned about some issues and opportunities that may not apply to you yet. The legal section should take you through this time of life and into the next, and help you get things in place as your life changes.

Follow us online at our Web site www.nowgetittogether.com, where you can submit questions and get answers to common scenarios.

It's time to get out there, start saving, build up your credit history, get those legal documents, and make smart financial decisions.

It's your life; now live it well!

Index

1% rule 25
401k plan 68-70, 99-100
80/20 rule 35-36
Adjustable-Rate Mortgages 87
amortization 89
annual percentage rate 51-53, 89
annuities 106-107
asset allocation 108-109
assets 44
auto loans 57
benchmarking investments 116
bonds 103-104
borrower 44
buying a home 83
capital loss and gain 98
car insurance 80
car leases 77
car loans 74-76
cash flow:
        inflow 23-25, 36
        outflow 25-30, 36-38
cash instruments 104-105
certificate of deposit 95-96
checking accounts 94-95, 99
combination loans 87
compound interest 32-33, 46
conservator 135
Consolidated Omnibus Budget Reconciliation Act 67
credit 32, 45-46, 50
credit cards:
        and debt 56-58
        interest rates 55, 57
        terms and conditions 53-55
        choosing 51-52
credit reports 48-49
credit score 48-50
debt 32, 44-45, 56-58
deductibles 65-66, 78
deferment of loans 62
defined benefit plans 68
depreciating assets 74
disability insurance 71
diversification 109-110
dividends 98
dollar cost averaging 110
durable financial power of attorney 121, 122-127
earthquake insurance 80
employee stock ownership plans 70
exchange-traded funds 106
executor 125, 134
expenses, reduction of 37-38
Fair Housing Act 83
Federal Deposit Insurance Corp. 96, 105
FHA loan 87
financial agent 124
flood insurance 80
forbearance of loans 62
guardian 132-133
healthcare power of attorney 121, 127
health insurance 64-67
Health Insurance Portability and Accountability Act 128
health savings account (HSA) 66
homeowner's insurance 79
individual retirement arrangement 99-100
inflation risk 102
installment debt 44
interest 46, 48, 98
intestate 136
investing steps 102-111
investment accounts 99
investment risk 102
lender 44
life insurance 71-72
living will 121, 127, 129

living with parents   81-82
oney market accounts   95
mortgages   85-89
mutual funds   105-106
overdraft protection   94-95
profit-sharing plans   71
renter's insurance   79
renting a home   82-83
required minimum distribution   100
retirement accounts   99-100
retirement plans   68-71
revolving debt   44
secured debt   44

spending accounts   72
stock indexes   115
stocks   103
student loans   59-62
tax-deferred accumulation   70
taxes on investments   116-117
time vs. things challenge   13-14
trustee   134-135
umbrella insurance   80
unsecured debt   44
VA loan   87
vesting   69
wills   131-136

Acknowledgments

Our sincere thanks to Eva Williams, Meg Hermann, Lori Kennemore, Brian McDowell, Dot Bolton, Tripp Griffin, and the friends and supporters of *Get It Together*.

About the Authors

Shannon "Shay" Jones Prosser (CDFA® & CCRR®) was a young, single person working at a software company when she began saving for retirement.
She wanted to know more about how best to save and how to plan, so she began reading everything she could get her hands on—books, magazines, online articles and calculators.
In 2006, she decided to turn a passion into a career and joined a major brokerage house as a financial advisor. She spent her first years in the financial industry, building a career around educating clients.
As more and more friends came to her for advice on how to secure their own futures, she realized that there was a greater need. She left the brokerage world to focus her efforts on financial education.

Hallie Gabor Hawkins (JD, CCRR®) followed a liberal arts undergraduate education by plunging into a tough job market. She began working in the mortgage industry and also worked in health insurance and life insurance before earning her law degree.
She practiced law for a while, gaining experience in broad legal issues that ranged from estate planning to real estate closings, debt consolidation, and many other complex issues. Her move to Charlotte brought her to a large corporation—and back to her mortgage 'roots'. She experienced 'downsizing' and started her own business, drawing on that rich background earned over a succession of diverse careers.

As fate would have it, a well-timed e-mail from Hallie to Shay about financial planning issues sparked a running conversation. Several conversations later, the two founded *Get It Together*. Through their company, Shay and Hallie have dedicated themselves to helping people take control of their legal and financial lives.

This is their first book.

Look for other real-life money guides from
Get It Together
for these life passages:

Credit

Marriage

Baby

Retirement

Divorce

Widowhood

Learn more at
http://get-it-together-today.com/